The Dance of Life

To Cherie,
who has helped
me save my life.

Pat Rielus

The Dance of Life

PERSPECTIVES

Pat Piety

To order additional copies of this book, contact:
Xlibris LLC
1-888-795-4274
www.Xlibris.com
Orders@Xlibris.com
142374

Contents

Epitaph

My genius was so small,
it was invisible to all but me.
Smaller than a mattress pea,
it dogged my nights and filled
my days with longing to be
something grander than I was—
something I could only see
in dreams.
But, still, it taunted me.

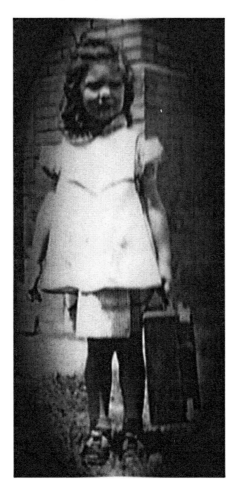

To Begin With...

When I was growing up, my mother used to laughingly refer to me as "Sarah Bernhardt" because of my tendency to overreact to life's little vicissitudes. Apparently, I haven't changed a lot over the years. Contrary to what some observers believe, I maintain that we "drama queens" are not faking it. Whatever it is that enables some people to cruise through life on a relatively even keel must be missing in our genetic makeup, although with years of therapy, self-help books and support groups, I have made some halting progress toward taking life's ups and downs with a degree of equanimity. But I am still capable of large mood swings, depending on the day, the time of year, the ambient temperature and humidity, a chance remark by a friend or stranger, or any number of things that would probably not even rise to the level of consciousness for most people.

A few years ago, it struck me that this tendency to see the events of my life in a totally positive or negative pattern could be compared to looking through a kaleidoscope: The facts, like the colored rocks in that fascinating toy, remain the same, but the pattern they make can change dramatically with a turn of the wheel. On days when I'm down, I look at them and tell myself, "No one has ever loved me. I can never do anything right. My life has been a failure. The future is grim." On other days, when the wheel has turned, I may say, "I've been extraordinarily blessed. I have a lot of friends. I've accomplished several things that I'm proud of. There is hope for the future." Probably all of us do that at times, at least a little bit.

The thought also occurred to me some years ago that I could tell the story of my life in terms of a single object, using a kind of word association to dredge up all of the significant events related in my memory to a particular object over time. For example, in "Shoes," the first essay of this collection, I started with a pair of baby shoes my parents had bronzed as bookends and followed the thread all the way to the present day. When I asked my freshman composition students to use this device, they came up with some fascinating essays about their lives. I'll bet you could, too.

My original intention was to write a series of brief, relatively light-hearted autobiographical essays. But as I got deeper into the project, I found myself gravitating toward more abstract concepts like "Motherhood," and the essays grew longer and, sometimes, darker. I considered going back to try to standardize them a bit, but ultimately I decided against it.

After reading some of the first essays, a friend suggested that I scatter a few of my poems throughout the collection, too, so I took her advice. Besides, the poems tell something about my relationships with men, a subject on which I wrote and discarded about half a dozen drafts, for reasons I'll leave the reader to surmise. In addition to the poems, I decided to include two stories—"Thursday" and "The Game"—that I had written more than 30 years ago.

By this time I was on a roll, so I threw in a few relevant photos from the collection of thousands I have always been planning to catalog before I die. After all, the rocks in a kaleidoscope vary in shape, size and color. If they were more uniform, the patterns would be less interesting. And, besides, since I am almost 75 years old as I write these words, I'm going for broke. I may not have time to write another book.

So the essays, poems, stories and pictures in this book are like colored rocks in the kaleidoscope of my life. Often, persons and events mentioned in one essay will be repeated, enlarged upon, or viewed from a different perspective in another. I suspect the pattern that emerges as one continues to read will be different for each reader, and no one can say which one is definitive.

My eldest daughter, a law professor, teaches a course called "Evidence," in both law school and medical school. Being an expert on this subject, she assures me that memory is very unreliable: Even when we are dead sure about what happened, she says, sometimes we are dead wrong. That's probably one reason that, no matter how hard we try, we can never fully understand ourselves, let alone anyone else. We can only try to make some sense of the dance of life through the stories we tell, based on our memories, however unreliable they may be. So that is what I have tried to do in this collection. Thanks for letting me share my stories with you. Enjoy.

Shoes

A long time ago, when I was a little girl, our family owned a pair of bookends made of baby shoes. When I was a little older, my parents told me these were my first shoes, which they had taken to be bronzed so they would always have something to remind them of those wonderful days of my infancy. Over the next few years, I suspect they sometimes looked at those shoes and longed for the good old days. After awhile, the thin bronze coating on the shoes began to wear off and you could see the cracked white leather underneath. I don't know what happened to them eventually, but thinking about them made me realize I could pretty much tell the story of my life in terms of shoes.

I don't remember wearing those baby shoes, of course, nor do I remember another famous pair that I wore when my parents, Pentecostal evangelists, traveled around the midwest in the 1940s holding "revivals" in churches along U.S. Route 66. But several people I met in later years said, "I remember you in your little white cowboy boots, standing up there on the altar, singing those children's choruses!" I think I had my fifteen minutes of fame early in life.

I do remember, however, a pair of wooden shoes my parents bought me during a trip to Holland, Michigan, when I was about four years old. They had been hand-carved by a man who sat working in the shoe store window, and I delighted in clunking around in them for several months, showing them off to the neighbor kids. When my feet grew out of them, my mother painted them blue, decorated them with flower decals, and hung them on the kitchen wall. Today they hang in the dining room of my youngest daughter, a lawyer in Enid, Oklahoma.

While I enjoyed those chunky wooden shoes, I definitely did not like the ugly brown oxfords my mother made me wear when we settled down in Waxahachie, Texas, so I could go to first grade. The oxfords, she assured me, would correct my flat feet, and I would be glad of that someday. All I knew was that Linda and Barbara, the two most popular girls in first grade, wore pretty little patent leather slippers with lacy white socks to school, while I had to wear those dorky oxfords. I would often look at those girls and wonder how they managed to stay so clean and tidy all day in their frilly little pinafore dresses while my barrettes had long since fallen out of my now-tangled hair, my belt had torn loose from my dress, and my socks had slipped way down into my ugly brown shoes. Clearly, Linda and Barbara were privy to some fashion secret that had passed me by. To this day, I still have trouble keeping a sharp crease in my slacks.

Somehow, though, I survived first grade and by the time I was in elementary school I was wearing brown-and-white saddle oxfords and penny loafers, like the other kids. Saddle oxfords were too much like my orthopedic shoes to ever have a lot of appeal for me, but penny loafers were cool—you could actually put a shiny penny in the pocket on the top of each shoe—mad money, in case you ever needed some for the gum ball machine. On Sundays, when I went to church in the pretty outfits my mother had made for me on her Singer Sewing machine, I got to wear patent leather slippers like Linda and Barbara had worn, but I still had an unfortunate tendency to let my socks slip down in my shoes.

During those years, my mother was prohibited from wearing makeup, earrings, or too-revealing dresses by the strict attitudes toward "worldliness" that prevailed in the Assemblies of God movement, so she poured all her pent-up sensuality into shoes. She had great legs, and a collection of attractive—though not too overtly sexy—high heels which showed them off. Although my mother and I went through some stormy years with each other—actually, about half a century of stormy years, to be more precise—two things I always enjoyed were listening to her sing and play, and watching her move around gracefully in those high heels.

By the time I reached my early teens, I had fallen for high heels myself—a love affair that has outlasted all the ones I've had with members of the opposite sex over the years. When I saw those flaming red pumps with cut-out toes in the store window, I immediately experienced an aching longing that wouldn't go away until they were mine. I had never liked bobby sox much, and with the shift to high heels, I abandoned socks altogether for nylon hose, which I thought were much more flattering to my legs. Although I didn't wear heels to Belleville High School, I always wore hose, and I remember some of the girls at school asking me why I was so dressed up. By my junior year, though, most of them were wearing hose, too, with the Capezio ballet slippers that were so popular in the 1950s.

I liked the Capezios, but heels were still my true love, and my passion for them must have been somewhat contagious, because when I was about fifteen, my maternal grandfather—a stern, German carpenter famous for his lack of public displays of affection—shocked the whole family by taking me on a shopping trip from his home in Collinsville, Illinois, to downtown St. Louis to buy me a pair of shoes. This crusty old man, who had been mean to my mom when she was growing up and had refused to attend the weddings of seven of his eight adult children, patiently tromped with me from store to store until I found the perfect pair—three-inch black patent leather pumps with white buckskin trim. And without batting an eye, he shelled out more for them than my dad earned in a day of preaching. If you're into Freudian analysis, I guess you could read a lot into that.

For the next half century—through two marriages, the births of my three daughters, numerous relationships, homes in five states and various stints as a teacher and writer/editor, I never tired of prancing around in heels—not stripper-high or the freaky stilt-like shoes with platforms that are currently all the rage, but three inches, at the lowest. I loved feeling tall and strong, with my long, well-muscled legs stretching down to slim ankles and the high arches I had developed thanks to Mama's insistence on those orthopedic oxfords.

As for Mom, though, the time came when her feet were too swollen and her balance too unsteady for her to wear heels any more. Once, when she was in her 80s and I went to take her out to dinner after working all day in high heels, she looked down at my feet and said, "I hate you for being able to wear those shoes." Even though she couldn't wear them any more, she kept a pair of maroon heels in her shoe bag on the closet door until the sad day, when she was almost 90 years old, that I had to take her to the nursing home. I guess that pair of shoes was her way of keeping hope alive.

In the last few years before I retired, I began to experience a significant amount of pain in the balls of my feet and I developed an annoying numbness in my toes that persists to this day. During my last year of full-time work, I started wearing heels less often. My co-workers were shocked. "Where are your high heels?" they would ask. In the years since my retirement, I have literally let myself down slowly, wearing two-inch heels for special occasions, but going around most of the time now in wedgies or flip-flops. Sometimes, in winter, I even wear a pair of brown shoes that—come to think of it—look disturbingly similar to those clunky brown oxfords of my grade school days. But I still have a pair of shiny black three-inch pumps with ankle straps on the shelf in my closet, just in case.

Cars

The other day when I was tooling along on I-170 at about about 65 miles an hour, a guy in a sporty little red convertible with the top down sped by me on the left, crossing in front of me to get to the Forest Park exit. It all happened so quickly that I didn't get a chance to see his face, but I caught a glimpse of the back of his bald, rather large head.

"Aha!" I thought, "Another man going through mid-life crisis. He's probably recently divorced and dating a little cutie about half his age."

Of course I could have been dead wrong. That driver might have been a dedicated family man, racing to the hospital for the birth of his first grandchild. But I think you'll agree that cars can tell a lot about people: Some folks use them as status symbols, some for power, and some, like my first husband, simply as a way to get from point A to point B. My own relationship with cars is more complex.

For a good part of my life, when my parents were Pentecostal evangelists, the car was my home. It was the 1940s, and no one had thought about seat belts yet, so I had free range over the whole car. Sometimes I sat up front between my parents as we sped along U. S. Route 66, pretending that the radio grille was a piano and I a talented pianist and singer. Sometimes I would lie on the narrow ledge behind the back seat, watching the road unravel, snake-like, behind us. But most of the time I dozed or sat on my crib mattress, which my parents had wedged between the front and back seats, watching the landscape go by and trying to peer in lighted windows when we passed through small towns at night.

In 1946, when my parents settled down in Collinsville, Illinois, so they could pastor a church in East St. Louis, I discovered another neat thing about cars. We often gave parishioners a ride to church, and sometimes the change that the kids had brought for the Sunday School offering plate must have slipped out of their hands, because every once in awhile I found nickels and dimes, and even quarters, on the back seat and the floor. Before long, I learned how to remove that seat and found what I came to think of as my secret bank.

The next year, when I was almost nine years old, my brother was born. My mother suffered from postpartum depression, bordering on psychosis, and relations between the two of us deteriorated seriously. That's when I discovered that the car was an excellent place to cry my eyes out without anyone noticing. At that age, I still believed in a God who would help me make straight A's or hit a home run in the softball games, so I did a lot of praying in the the back of the car that God would put things back the way they used to be. I liked to imagine the car was a giant swing, in which God was rocking me to sleep, like a baby.

I'm sure my dad noticed my unhappiness—we were all pretty miserable around then, even my baby brother, who cried with the colic every night at 6 p.m. like clockwork—so perhaps that's why, shortly after my ninth birthday, Dad taught me to drive. We lived on a hill on the outskirts of town, below which was a notorious blacktop road. Local legend had it that the Wortman Gang had bumped off one or more enemies and dumped them on the roadside in the dark down there in the past. In daylight, though, it was a pretty safe road, with very little traffic, so one Sunday afternoon when we were driving home from church, Dad invited me to get behind the wheel of our brand-new Chevrolet sedan. He explained the H-formation of the gears on the shift wand, which was mounted on the steering column, and he cautioned me to let the clutch out slowly while gradually pushing down on the gas. And off we hopped.

That first ride was pretty jerky, but I soon got the hang of it. I practiced driving up and down the driveway behind our house for a year or so, and by the time my brother was a toddler, I was giving him and my friends rides all over the neighborhood. Once when we were out driving, I saw that we were almost out of gas, so I pulled in to a station and asked the attendant to give me a quarter's worth of gas— about a gallon back then. When I saw the gas meter racing up toward a dollar, I hollered, "Hey, I said a quarter's worth!" The young attendant said sheepishly, "I thought you said a dollar's worth." When I explained that all of us in the car together could only come up with a quarter, he let us go without calling the cops. The next day, my dad went back and paid the station the difference.

I don't know what my parents were thinking. I would never have let my own children drive a car at that age. Ironically, though, I never had an accident until shortly after I got my license. Driving in the Thanksgiving Day parade in high school, I was waving to some friends on the sidewalk and rammed into the car in front of me. There was more damage to my pride than to the car or its occupants, and I tried to keep the accident a secret from my parents, thinking that I could pay for the damage out of my earnings from working part-time in the credit office of Famous-Barr department store in St. Louis. I didn't realize how much bodywork cost, though, until I came home from school one day to find my dad holding a letter from the insurance company of the car's owner. I guess Dad could see how scared I was. "If it ever happens again, Honey," he said kindly, "be sure to tell me right away so we can file a claim with the insurance company." It never happened again.

In high school I occasionally got to drive my mother's car to school or around town. She had a little second-hand Henry J, a four-cylinder Ford that had bombed on the market just a year or two after being introduced. It was a tin can, but fun for kids. Once when I threw a spaghetti dinner party for my physics class, several of us piled into the Henry J after dinner and went swooping up and down the steep dip in the road behind my house in Belleville, where our family had moved a couple of years before. Such fun!

The less said the better about the second-hand Pontiac with the steeply sloping back that my boyfriend drove when I was in high school. (He was six years older and had dropped out of school after junior high.) If you've ever seen a movie called "The Last Picture Show," you probably know what I'm talking about. I will only tell you that, when I was 14, we ran away in that car to get married but had to return home when we found out the state of Arkansas had recently enacted a law requiring a three-day wait and blood tests for marriage licenses. But that's a whole other story.

Despite my love affair with cars. It would be several more years before I got one of my own. Married at 19, I had three kids before I was 24, and while they were growing up we had a succession of mostly unmemorable Valiants in which we took some very fun road trips—twice to California, once to Hilton Head, S. Carolina, and once to a national park on Lake Huron, in Canada, among others. On one camping trip to a state park, my oldest daughter, who has never been the outdoor type, spent the whole weekend in the back of our Plymouth station wagon, reading historical romances. She only came out for meals.

In 1966, when I was teaching third grade in O'Fallon, Illinois, I finally purchased the first car that I could call my very own. For $300 I bought a big, mint-green, bosomy 1955 Cadillac with cushiony seats and automatic everything. To my unending delight, the radio dial would automatically seek out local stations and the windows would go up and down at the press of a button. For a couple of years, I was in heaven with that car. I would have been happy to live in it. When it developed a problem that seemed too costly to fix, I sadly donated it to a worthy young man in East St. Louis who fixed it up and sold it for $75.

In the 1980's, when the girls were in their teens and I had been divorced from their father for a year or two, I met a man who was destined to become my second husband. The marriage was memorable mainly for the road trips we took in his little silver Honda. I think maybe I actually fell in love with his car. It was my first intimate relationship with a car that had a cup holder, a tape player, and seats that would recline all the way. Moreover, he had added a wastebasket to make it a true home away from home. On our honeymoon, playing Earl Klugh's "Layla" over and over, we drove down the east coast of Mexico, across the center of the country to Cuernavaca, and up the west coast to Zijuatanejo, a small fishing village near the Club Med resort of Ixtapa. I loved every mile of the adventure, but my new husband, who came down with a bad case of Montezuma's Revenge, was less captivated by the experience. Although we didn't admit it at the time, our marriage was almost over by the end of the honeymoon. When we got divorced a couple of years later, I got custody of the Honda.

In the years since then, I've had only one car worth mentioning: A green Mitsubishi with leather seats and a sunroof that made me feel very cool and rather glamorous for a woman in her fifties. For the past decade, though, I've driven a very serviceable but boring Toyota Camry like you would expect an old-maid school teacher to drive. I kept scraping the wheel covers off on the curb, so I finally threw them away, but I'm thinking about painting flowers or flames on the wheels, just to add a little excitement. On the other hand, if there is a rich relative hiding somewhere among my very large family, and if that person decides to include me in the will, and if I'm lucky enough to outlive him or her, I may just buy a little red Mercedes convertible to tool around in before I die.

Books

I cannot talk about my life with books without talking about my dad, Paul V. Chamless. He introduced me to books, and his life, like my

own, is full of what might appear upon first glance to be glaring contradictions. To say that he was both a Pentecostal preacher and an expert in rare books for most of his life doesn't begin to sum it up. "Humanitarian," "free-thinker," "equal rights advocate," "student of American history," even "entrepreneur," are some terms that come to mind, but they are not ones that could easily have been predicted, given his background.

Born in Dripping Springs, Texas, in 1913, Dad was the eldest of eleven children of a dirt-poor itinerant Pentecostal preacher and the former mistress of a gambling man (so family legend has it). At the age of 15, he had already left home and was working in a broom factory in Lubbock, Texas, when the pastor of the local church, who knew his dad, surprised him by announcing that "Brother Paul is going to preach the sermon next Sunday night." As Dad told it, the thought of preaching had never entered his head up to that point, but shortly after his first sermon, he took to the road, staying in members' homes and preaching at little congregations all around Texas, Oklahoma, and the central U.S. for the next few years.

He wasn't very good at it at first—a fact he learned by overhearing a conversation in a home where he was staying. The family had put him up in a bed on the sleeping porch and they thought he was still asleep. "He's not much of a preacher," one of them said, 'but he's a nice boy.'" Dad kept at the preaching, though, and gradually he got better. He was a firm believer in the Bible, and preaching was better than working in a broom factory or pulling cotton, another job he had already held among the few that were open to a young man with almost no formal schooling and even less sophistication. I thought for years that he had made it through at least a couple of years of high school because he once said something about having been good at the high jump when he was a teenager, but my stepmother says his schooling didn't extend beyond third or fourth grade. He never got over his embarrassment about this deficiency, but by the time I was old enough to notice, his knowledge of literature, philosophy, and psychology would rival that of many college professors. And he was an expert on rare Americana. But in the beginning, he just loved to read.

Uncle Wes, Dad's younger brother, told me that when their father had made an especially vicious attack on Dad while he was growing up, Dad faked running away from home by hiding in the attic for a week or more. His younger siblings took turns sneaking food up to him and, as Uncle Wes said, "He had a stack of westerns up there, so he was happy."

By the time Dad met my mother in 1935, he was still pretty wet behind the ears. Mom, a gifted musician and an Assemblies of God minister herself, had a year of college under her belt and was pastoring her own church, which was meeting in a rented room in a tobacco barn in Paducah, Kentucky. Dad came to hold a "revival" at her church, but he had some misgivings when he heard her express what he considered radical ideas. She suggested that when the Apostle Paul said women shouldn't be preachers, he was just stating his own opinion. Dad told me he had been afraid Mom might be going to hell for suggesting that every word of the Bible wasn't divinely inspired. But he overcame his reservations and they were married within a few months of meeting, and Mom gave up her congregation to join Dad on the road. Although she would never admit it, the fact that Dad was "tall, dark and handsome" like the romance heroes of the times might have had something to do with her decision. At six feet, he looked a bit like Clark Gable with a hint of Burt Parks' nose, and he prided himself on keeping his weight at a steady 175 all his life. No stranger to physical labor, he was nevertheless fastidious about his appearance, often changing his white cotton long-sleeved shirts two or three times a day. I still remember seeing Mom dip the collars and cuffs in a cup of starch before she ironed them to make sure they were stiff enough to satisfy him.

My parents pastored a couple of churches in Texas for about five years after their marriage, but in 1941, when I was less than three years old, they went on the road again, taking me with them. For the next three years we had a great life, traveling U.S. Route 66 or riding the Missouri-Kansas-Texas railroad ("Katy," for short), and staying in small hotels or people's homes. Dad preached and Mom played the piano and sang for services six nights a week and twice on Sunday. I got to know all of Dad's stories by heart, often whispering the punch lines to those sitting too close to me. One of his most memorable sermons was about a little boy who had fallen in an oil-well hole being drilled in Texas. "Daddy get me out of here!" the little boy had cried, while the oilmen worked furiously, but vainly, to save him. All of us sinners are like that little boy, Dad told the weeping members of the congregation as tears ran down his own cheeks. But, unlike that poor little boy, we have a Father in Heaven who can reach down and pull us out of the well of sin and despair.

During our time on the road, and for a couple of years afterwards, when Mom taught piano and Dad was dean of men at Southwestern Bible Institute in Waxahachie, Texas, Dad rented a woman's attic in Collinsville, Illinois, where my mother's family lived, to store the books he collected everywhere we stopped. In the fall of 1945, when my parents settled down to co-pastor a church on 84th Street in East St. Louis, Mom's carpenter brothers built a tiny three-room home for us and Dad soon put a floor in the detached garage so he could use it to store his books. Later, when we added a two-story wing that included a more formal library, Dad continued to use the garage for overflow. He had taught himself to tint the prints that he found in old county Atlases with permanent transparent watercolors, and he was tracking down the heirs of the people whose ancestral homes were pictured in the atlases to sell them the prints. He had also taught himself to cut mats, so the converted garage served as an excellent workroom. Later, he bought equipment and learned to make frames, as well.

Everywhere we went, Dad searched the newspaper ads for estate sales, and he never passed up a used book store in any town we visited. A lot of times, the rest of the family sat in the car and waited. My little brother, who was born when I was almost nine, is famous for the very first sentence he uttered, which occurred after Dad had dragged us along on one of his extensive bookstore explorations: "Bye-bye, huh-uh," he protested.

At first, Dad didn't know good literature from bad or rare books from ones that were merely old. He just knew what he liked. But over time he learned how to identify collectors' items and developed a laser-like skill for zeroing in on writing that was truly great. By the time I can remember him, he no longer bore much resemblance to that young man who had feared my mother was going to hell for doubting that Paul's opinions were divinely inspired. Two things that never changed about him, though, were his humility and his compassion, and he did his best to pass those values on to me. From as far back as I can remember, Dad deliberately exposed me to books that he thought would enlarge my world view and increase my empathy for my fellow human beings. When I read *The Grapes of Wrath* in eighth grade, he explained that the family in the novel resembled his own. His poverty-stricken childhood in Texas and Oklahoma had left him with a lasting empathy for the poor, the uneducated, and the downtrodden. His political inclinations were definitely socialist, but he never exhibited a dedication to any political party or ideology, reserving instead a healthy level of skepticism about the motivations of politicians of all stripes.

Among Dad's expressed beliefs was also a distaste for war and violence. One of my earliest memories is of his taking me to a reading of *The Story of Ferdinand*, by Munro Leaf. Published in 1936, just nine months before the outbreak of the Spanish Civil War, it was viewed as pacifist propaganda by some critics because Ferdinand, a bull who was groomed to be the aggressor in a Spanish bullfight, refused to fight, preferring to lie down in the middle of the ring and smell the flowers.

Racism was also anathema to Dad. He said he had once watched a black man in a Texas post office go to the back of the line every time a white person entered. "I don't want to live in a state that treats people that way," he said. Of course my mom's home state of Illinois had plenty of racism of its own, but it was perhaps less overt to a white out-of-stater. One of the first books Dad gave me was *Those Plummer Children*, by Christine Noble Govan, in which the white children of a southern judge played elaborate games of pretend with the children of their African-American servants. Recently, I relocated a copy of the book and was pleased to find that although it contains some elements of outdated paternalism, the author's genuine affection and respect for all the children is never in doubt. I'm sure what Dad wanted me to see was black and white children playing together.

Another author that Dad introduced to me very early in life was the African-American poet Paul Laurence Dunbar. I didn't hear much, if anything, about Dunbar in college literature classes, probably in part because many of his poems were in dialect. But he also wrote lyrically beautiful poems in what English teachers call Standard English. I have read many books by African-American authors since then, but I don't believe any writer was better at expressing the pain of being black in America than Dunbar, with poems like "We Wear the Mask" and "Sympathy." In fact, Maya Angelou took the title of her autobiography, *I Know Why the Caged Bird Sings*, from "Sympathy." Nor has anyone, in my view, done a better job of picturing the sweetness of parenthood or the sorrow of losing a child than Dunbar did in poems like "Little Brown Baby With Spa'klin' Eyes" and "Puttin' de Baby Away." Years later, when I was living in Dayton, Ohio, I was delighted to discover that the public library was named for Dunbar and he was buried there in the same cemetery as the Wright brothers. One of my favorite activities was to sit in my car in that cemetery on the hilltop and read a book while eating my lunch.

Dad's sympathies extended not just to the poor and the racially shunned, but to anyone who lived outside of society's rigid norms. I'm not sure when he slipped a copy of Radclyffe Hall's *Well of Loneliness* on my bookshelf, but it was well before I went to college. Although I wasn't aware of knowing any lesbians at the time, I was already being primed to feel compassion for homosexuals.

One of Dad's choices which made a lasting impression on me was *Around the World in 11 Years*, by Patience, Richard, and John Abbe, published in 1938, the year I was born. Children of a professional photographer, they traveled around the world with their parents, living a bohemian life. Sometimes they hobnobbed with the rich and famous, staying in mansions, and sometimes they were out on the street when their funds ran low. The book contained photos of the children in various locations, including a German beer hall and a nude beach in some Scandinavian country. Since our church forbade alcohol and American society shunned nude bathing, that book was deliciously intriguing to me. But what really captured my imagination was the travel and adventure. No doubt it influenced my own love of travel and my notoriously reckless attitude about financial security in later life. (I lost track of that book for many years, but after my marriage to Harold Piety, the father of my three wonderful daughters, I talked to him about it several times. While we were on a road trip to New Orleans in 1977, just prior to our separation, Harold found it on the shelf in a second-hand bookstore and bought it for me. I guess it was kind of like a wedding present in reverse, and a reminder that, wherever our paths might lead us individually in the future, we still had a strong bond of shared experience.)

Over the years, Dad slowly evolved into a closet freethinker, but while he privately rejected the biblical story of creation, he still believed passionately in Jesus's teachings about humility and compassion. So he was faced with a dilemma: He didn't have the education or credentials for the life of a professor or a psychologist, which might have suited him. Moreover, our whole lives revolved around the closed circle of our denomination. He would have encountered significant challenges in trying to extricate himself from it. And despite the fact that Mom had been the more liberal thinker when they met, her views had not evolved along with his. So he made the only compromise that seemed possible: After he came to pastor in East St. Louis, I don't think he ever preached a sermon that wasn't related in some way to The Sermon on the Mount. Hellfire and brimstone just weren't part of his repertoire.

Dad loved women—perhaps in part because he had six flamboyant, flirtatious sisters and a mother with a colorful past who adored him—and women obviously loved him back. They tended to confide in him, but so did men. He was such a sympathetic, non-judgmental listener that he learned many people's deepest secrets, which may be one reason he was fascinated by human sexual behavior. His library was brimming with books on the subject by Havelock Ellis, Sigmund Freud, Alfred Kinsey, and others.

My childhood reading choices were probably significantly different from those of my peers, not only because they included anthropological tomes with titles like "Sexual Practices of Indigenous Peoples," but also because many of the books I read were very old, and some were downright obscure. I never read a new book and rarely went to the library. Why should I, when I was surrounded by books? And although I can see clearly now that Dad had a huge influence on the person I became, he never insisted that I read anything in particular. It is only looking back that I see a pattern in the volumes that appeared on my bedroom shelves.

When I was a teenager, Dad gave me a book called *Maidcraft, A Guide to the Art of Housekeeping*, which contained detailed information about the proper placement of silverware for a formal dinner party and how to make beds with hospital corners and watercress sandwiches with the crusts removed. Another book, the title of which I have forgotten, although I can still see the illustrations in my mind's eye, contained tips on grooming and illustrations on how to apply makeup. While one could jump to the conclusion from those choices that Dad was a male chauvinist, he was in fact a vocal advocate for equal rights. When one of my uncles called a woman a slut because he had slept with her, Dad's response was, "Then I guess that makes you a slut, too, doesn't it?"

One book Dad gave me in my teens, called *The Book Without a Name: Being the 18th Century Journal of an Unmarried English Lady to her Natural Son,* seemed pretty obviously to represent his views on women, sex, and a host of other subjects. Allegedly, it was the authentic diary of a wealthy noblewoman that had been passed down in the family for generations and was finally made available for publication by one of her heirs. While she loved her child's father, the author didn't believe in marriage—thought it was a kind of bondage for women. She wasn't sold on religion, either, as evidenced by a chapter titled "Truth! Be More Sacred to Me Than Religion!" Nor was she enamored of royalty, or war, as indicated by another chapter, "Kings Are Not Worth the Spilling of Blood." It was not until I re-read that book in the process of writing this essay that I began to suspect why it had appeared on my shelf when it did. When I was 14, I had eloped with a boy from our church who was 6 years my senior to Piggott, Arkansas, where we had heard that girls under 16 could marry without parental consent. To our disappointment, we found when we got there that we would have to wait three days for blood tests. Since we didn't have enough money, we had to come back with our tails between our legs and I was forbidden from ever seeing that boy again. Looking back on that time and re-reading *The Book Without a Name,* I suspect my dad was trying to tell me there were other ways of viewing sex and marriage than the ones that currently prevailed in society, and in our church.

Dad frequently talked about how he hoped I would become a doctor, lawyer, or other professional someday, so when I decided as a senior in high school to major in architecture, he was thrilled. Upon the advice of an architect friend, he encouraged me to apply to Oklahoma State University, an institution within my parents' means that was well-known for its architecture school. Dad drove me down to the campus himself, and I discovered that he had brought along a box of books for me to keep in my room. I have to confess that I never finished reading William James's *The Varieties of Religious Experience,* but I still enjoy Lin Yutang's *The Wisdom of China and India,* which was also in that box. Once I started classes, I remember being struck by the fact that many of the authors my professors referred to were ones whose works Dad had read to us at the dinner table or placed on my bedroom shelves when I was growing up.

When I decided to change my major to English at the end of the first semester, Dad couldn't hide his disappointment. "If you're

going to major in English, you might as well come home and go
to the community college," he said. It was apparent that he didn't
understand why anyone needed to go to a university to read books,
since he had been doing that all his life without benefit of classroom
or teacher. Although I never doubted Dad's love, I have often felt that
I failed him by not going into one of the professions, and I have always
regretted that Alzheimer's kept him from ever knowing that his three
Piety granddaughters became a law professor, a philosophy professor,
and a partner in a law firm. He would have been bursting with pride
if he had lived to see that two of them are published authors and
the youngest has handled legal appeals that have resulted in several
precedent-setting published opinions.

During my freshman year of college, Dad opened a used bookstore
called "Landmark Gallery" in a little building on 10th Street in East St.
Louis. When I came home that summer, I worked in the store while
he was out scouting for books. That store had a lasting impact on my
life, because it's where I met the man who would become the father
of my three daughters. Like Dad, Harold Piety was darkly handsome
and he loved books. What's more, he shared a birthday with my dad:
December 16. Harold was new in town, having just graduated from the
University of Illinois after four years in the U.S. Navy. A couple of weeks
before coming into the store, he had started a job as a sportswriter at
the now-defunct *East St. Louis Journal* (later the *Metro-East Journal*). He
was living in a rooming house a few blocks down the street and every
time he passed the store on the way home from work, he had wanted
to stop in, but he hadn't yet received a paycheck. Finally, he couldn't
resist the siren lure of books any longer and came in anyway—and
he stayed four hours. While he was there, Dad dropped by to check
on things. Sometime after I was married, I learned that Dad had
immediately gone home to my mother and told her, "The boy Pat's
going to marry is down in the bookstore."

The two men bonded instantly, and Dad never tired of telling
people, "I couldn't have a better son-in-law if I had hewn him out
with my own hands!" Although Harold was a professed atheist, when
Dad's preacher friends would ask him what kind of boy I was going
to marry, he got a big kick out of exclaiming, "He's the soul of piety!"
Dad performed our wedding ceremony within five months of Harold's
first visit to the bookstore, his voice shaking as he began with "Dearly
Beloved . . ." When we were divorced 20 years and three daughters
later, I was half afraid that I would lose my dad along with my husband.
But, without prompting, he assured me that although he didn't want to
have to take sides, if he had to do so, he would be on my side. Luckily,

he never had to be tested, as our divorce was amicable and Harold and I have remained friends to this day.

For a brief period during my marriage to Harold, Dad—perhaps emboldened by having an atheist for a son-in-law—actually did try to break out of preaching and make his living selling books and prints. First, he attended the Unitarian church in St. Louis, from which he moved on to the more adamantly non-religious Ethical Society. But Mom made all of our lives so miserable that, after a couple of years, he caved in to her constant importuning and accepted a position as pastor of a church in Sorento, a tiny town in central Illinois. Dad was popular not only with the congregation but also with many townspeople, and he ended up writing a regular column for the local newspaper. Mostly, his columns contained small observations about residents' gardens or cooking or other things to make them feel good, but he always ended with a proverb, a scripture, or a quotation from literature. As I page through a scrapbook of his columns, I find quotations within the first dozen pages from Chaucer, Whitman, Robert Browning, Pascal, Emerson, Tolstoi, and Coleridge.

After 34 passionate but rocky years of marriage, my mother divorced my dad. When Dad remarried a couple of years later, he lost his papers as an ordained minister of the Assemblies of God, since the church had only recently accepted divorce among its clergy and totally forbade remarriage. Meanwhile, Dad had already established a relationship with the Lovejoy Library at Southern Illinois University at Edwardsville as a freelance book scout, since the new satellite campus was still in the early stages of development and needed to build up its collection. Soon he became a full-time employee with the official title of "field representative," bringing in hundreds of books and tutoring members of the staff in the art of recognizing rare volumes. When Dad would bring back a collection from one of his book-buying tours, these employees would cull them out, relegating the ones the library didn't need to a used bookstore that had been established in the basement for that purpose.

It wasn't easy being a book scout, but Dad loved it. He had learned the hard way, he said, that when he went to look at a collection that was up for sale, he couldn't tell the owners which books were most valuable, because then they would want to hold those volumes back or try to jack up the price. Once he spent all day dividing a woman's collection into smaller and smaller piles as she debated how many she was willing to part with. Finally, after all his work, she decided that she didn't want to sell any of them. "She had just used me to find the valuable books for her," he said. He was so angry that he made sure to mix up all the piles before taking his leave.

After nearly two decades with SIUE, Dad's career there ended when he began to show signs of Alzheimer's. I had recently taken a job in the Public Affairs department of the Western Region Operations Center of American Express in Phoenix, and before his Alzheimer's got really bad, my stepmother would send him out to spend a week or two with me. Because my job was very demanding, I had to leave Dad at home alone for several hours every day. He could no longer read, so he had to find other ways of amusing himself. One evening when I came home from work he proudly gestured toward my bookshelves to indicate that he had dusted and rearranged all the books. He loved books not only for what was inside them, but for their physical presence. I have seen him stroke fine leather bindings and carefully separate the uncut rag-paper pages of old books with all the tenderness of a lover. In fact, I always thought that if I could find anything in life that I cared about as much as he loved books, I would be lucky, indeed. I'm not sure I ever did, beyond my own children. Unless it was Dad.

On July 4, 1989, after returning from a trip to the east coast with my stepmother, Dad sat down on the couch and died. I will always be grateful that I had quit my job in Phoenix in January of that year and returned to the St. Louis area to be near him and my mother, who was also ailing. During Dad's final six months, we had some precious hours together. He could no longer speak in full sentences, but he often managed, through gestures and phrases, to convey his feelings about the world around him. Gazing out my 11th-story window at the St. Louis Cathedral and the city skyline, he would smile and sweep his hand out broadly as if to say, "What a sight!" The last time he came to visit me, as we were standing by the elevator to go down to meet my stepmother in the lobby, I said, "I love you, Dad." When he didn't answer immediately, I asked, "Do you love me?" "More than ever," he replied. It was the last thing he ever said to me.

There were two memorial services for Dad—one in the little church that he and my stepmother had attended for several years, and one in the Lovejoy Library at SIUE. At that service, cowboy preachers and distinguished professors rubbed shoulders with a veritable cross-section of American society. My former husband, Harold, who had come back from Pennsylvania, read such a moving tribute to Dad that, by the time it was my turn, my hands were trembling and my voice was shaking. But I had something I wanted to read.

When Dad first learned he was getting Alzheimer's, he started making lists of all the people in his life that he wanted to thank, and he wrote some brief anecdotes about some of them in a journal. His punctuation and spelling had never been the best, and by the time he wrote these notes, his handwriting was spidery and his style was somewhat like that of a first-grade primer, so I will paraphrase his story here. Before I do, though, I should warn you that, although Dad was well aware of the fallacy of sweeping generalizations, his enthusiasm for life often prompted him to hyperbole. "You're the best daughter a daddy could ever have!" he used to exclaim, patting my cheek so hard I could feel my brains rattling—after which he would add thoughtfully, "but I guess most parents think that about their children." In telling the story of how he became a rare book expert, though, he could not resist giving himself over to both sweeping generalizations and hyperbole as he poured out his thanks to the man who had changed his life.

In the mid-1940s, after our permanent move to Illinois, Dad had spent a lot of time in a used bookstore across the river in St. Louis which was owned by a Jewish man named Keller. I'm not sure I ever knew his first name, although I heard Dad talk about him many times. During his visits to Mr. Keller's store, Dad often talked to the older man about his own collection, so one day Mr. Keller expressed an interest in coming to look at it. Spending less than an hour looking over Dad's books, he asked, "Do you want me to tell you the truth?" When Dad answered yes, he said, "You don't have one damn book that is worth anything." It was a crushing blow, Dad wrote, but he was heartened by the next words out of the man who was to become his mentor: "But you are *hooked* on books and you will never get over it, so I will teach you how to recognize rare books"—and he did. From this experience, Dad wrote, he learned "that Jews are the most helpful people in the world!"

Today, there are numerous volumes of Americana scattered throughout the Lovejoy Library at Southern Illinois University in Edwardsville containing bookplates honoring Dad's legacy. In addition, among the major collections of the Mercantile Library in St. Louis is the Paul V. Chamless Print Collection, containing approximately "1000 separate maps, prints of cities and towns, agricultural sciences, [and] American views."

After Dad's death, my stepmother gave me a few of his books—ones that he had especially loved. They are full of underlinings and comments in the margins, and occasional cryptic references to events in his life. In the front of the poetry books, he has listed the page numbers of his favorite poems. Whenever I read these books, I feel as if I'm having a conversation with him.

It is almost like having him back.

Breasts

My daddy was big brother to six gorgeous, fun-loving sisters. They favored big hats, colorful earrings, attention-getting clothes—and men. And the men loved them right back. I'm sure their appreciation of a good time was part of the reason men were attracted to them, but several of them also had *enormous* breasts.

As a child, I often marveled at these bountiful bosoms. Once when I was still a kid and Dad's baby sister, Billie Jo, had just given birth to her son, Doug, I watched spellbound as she pulled that incredible mammary out of her blouse to nurse him. I had never seen anything so big in my life. The baby's head was almost lost in it.

There was no question that the girls knew the value of their assets. Aunt Wanda Fay, who was a manicurist at the Missouri Athletic Club in St. Louis for several years and regularly dated its rich members, was seen more than once adjusting the twins in her industrial strength bra the way some men cup their crotches to assure themselves that the family jewels are still intact and securely stowed.

My mother, on the other hand, had very small breasts—too small for regulation bras, which didn't come in double-A or training sizes in those days, so her brassieres always had wrinkles in them. Perhaps to divert attention from them—or simply because she was a minister in a puritanical Pentecostal church—she tended to wear her clothes a size too big. You could scarcely tell she had anything up there.

As a little girl, I worried quite a bit about whether I would turn out like my mom or like my daddy's sisters, who seemed to have so much more fun. My dad must have heard me speculating about it because I remember him saying one time, "Aw, Honey, when they get old, they hang down to their knees." Despite his reassurance that little ones were OK, I continued to hope for the big ones until I finally had to concede that my mama's genes had won out.

When I was just beginning to bud, though, I had an experience that made me keenly aware of just how fascinating these chest adornments are to some men. It happened during a visit with friends, and it marked the first time I had to weigh alternatives to make a serious moral/ethical decision entirely on my own. My parents, overburdened with a toddler and a smart-alecky nine-year-old daughter, had sent me to stay with a woman who had cared for me as a baby. The husband was an oil field worker who, like many husbands of that era, played only a bit part in the daily drama of domestic life. He wasn't home a lot, and when he was there, he seldom had anything to say, but he was always good to me. One day, when I found myself alone with him, he pulled me between his knees to give me a hug, and as he did, his hands swept lightly over the tiny bumps on my chest. I'm pretty sure he thought I was oblivious to his copping a feel, but I knew instantly what had happened, and I was troubled—more for his wife than for myself. If I told her what he had done, I knew she would be upset. I really didn't want to cause him any trouble, but I felt very uncomfortable. Without letting on that I knew what he had done, I went for a long walk, shedding a few tears and trying to figure out what to do. In the end, I decided to keep mum and make sure I was never alone with him again. For the rest of the stay and subsequent visits to their home, he never committed another indiscretion. I'd like to think that what he did was a one-time, spur-of-the-moment failure of impulse control, but I'll never know for sure.

My breasts were a trouble to me in school, too. After they got a certain size, my mother donated a couple of her bras to me. Unlike today, when bras are carefully engineered showcases for the plastic surgeon's art, brassieres served primarily as protective covering back then, at least in my mother's view, so even though I couldn't fill them out, I had to wear them. "You don't really need a bra," my best friend in eighth grade said, pointing out the painfully obvious. Dressing for gym in high school was agonizing. Embarrassed by my flat chest and wrinkled bra, I tried to find ways of changing clothes without letting the other girls see them. To make matters worse, what I was missing on top was more than compensated for on the bottom. As a sophomore, I had a 25-inch waist and 40-inch hips. So I started wearing padded bras, rationalizing that they made my clothes fit better. This gave a considerable boost to my morale—except when it came to heavy petting. Out of necessity, I became an expert at devising clever ways to guide a boy's hand away from my chest, for fear a fistful of foam rubber would turn him off.

Despite this handicap, I managed to attract my share of boyfriends, as evidenced by the fact that I was married by the age of 19. Within three weeks of the wedding night I was pregnant and, to my utter delight (no pun intended), my breasts swelled to fill a B cup for the first time. But it wasn't until I began nursing that I realized the true purpose of those things on my chest. When my firstborn's tiny hands patted my bosom as she nursed contentedly, I felt like Mother Earth. I cried when I had to wean her to the bottle. Within three and half years, I had two more babies, and the pleasure of nursing them never got old.

But all good things must end. Eventually the babies went to bottles and my boobs returned to their normal, unimpressive size.

When the girls were little, my husband and I subscribed to *Playboy Magazine,* which my youngest daughter says was an example of irresponsible parenting. Those were the days before the girly magazines "went pink," as they said in the business, so the photos focussed mainly on legs and breasts, with pubic areas discreetly covered or airbrushed out. I said—*and I believed then*—that I read Playboy for the great interviews: Remember the one in which Jimmy Carter admitted he had committed adultery in his heart? Before I had my consciousness sufficiently raised, I thought the Playboy Philosophy sounded pretty good, too, although Hef's subsequently hedonistic life looks kind of pitiful now. But probably the main reason I liked to look at his magazine was to fantasize about being one of those Playmates with their beautiful breasts.

By the time my daughters were teenagers, their father suggested that if I really wanted bigger breasts, I should consider having enhancement surgery. I don't know why his suggestion hurt my feelings so much. After all, he had stuck with me through thick and thin, so to speak. But I couldn't help thinking he was wishing I would do it. Fat chance. I was 45 years old before I decided to mutilate my body enough to have my ears pierced. No way was I going to have some doctor tear up my chest to implant balloons. I had lived with foam and fiberfill since puberty, so I figured I would just go on making do with fantasy.

In the meantime, all the women I had looked up to were getting older, and an interesting thing was happening: My mother's bosom was beginning to grow fuller, while my aunts' once-magnificent racks were, indeed, starting to sag to their knees. (I can't *personally* verify this statement, but I can make a pretty educated guess, judging from the photo of a naked old tattooed lady several friends sent to me by email.)

One of my mother's favorite sayings when I was growing up was "Your time's coming!" This was usually said when I had done something to displease her, but seeing her bosom increase as she aged, I began to think there could be a *positive* side to her prediction.

Sure enough, a few years ago, when we were swimming in my youngest daughter's pool, she startled me by asking if I had undergone breast enlargement. This is the same daughter who thinks her parents were wrong to have *Playboy* lying around the house when she was growing up. I suspect she's right. For sure, there is much more to the women I know than what they carry on their chests. Still, I think Mother Nature has a wicked sense of humor. Now that it's no longer of any earthly use to me, I finally have the cleavage I always yearned for.

Music

One of my earliest memories is of riding in the front seat between my parents during the early 1940s, pretending that the radio grille was a piano and I the pianist as we cruised along U.S. Highway 66 from one religious "revival" to another. The Assemblies of God movement, in which both of my parents were ministers, was born of emotion and baptized in music, which is probably why my mother wound up being a lady preacher.

During a fall from grace during her late teens, Mom flirted briefly with an offer to travel with a dance band as singer/pianist, but God won out, and she joined the musical troupe of a traveling lady evangelist. Mom sang and played the piano, the guitar, the banjo, and even the mandolin on occasion, and through a totally unanticipated series of events, she found herself pastoring a small congregation in a rented room of a tobacco barn in Paducah, Kentucky, in the early 1930s. She even had her own radio program on a local station.

My parents met when Dad came to hold a revival for Mom in Paducah, and they were married within a few months. In later years, she claimed that he had married her because her talents as a musician were an asset to an evangelist like him, and there's no doubt her musical talent was an overwhelming component in her appeal. In many ways, she was a difficult woman, but no matter how angry we got with each other, or how much I thought I hated her at times, I never tired of listening to her play and sing. And while she remained faithful to her church for the rest of her life, the music she played and sang at home often harked back to the days when she had dreamed of traveling with that dance band. "Deep Purple," "Stormy Weather," "Smoke Gets In Your Eyes," and "St. Louis Blues" were staples of her in-house repertoire, along with a lesser-known but haunting melody called "Dancing on the Ceiling," about a distant lover who dances in the singer's dreams. This piece, not to be confused with the Lionel Richie production, was composed by Richard Rodgers for the 1930 musical, "Ever Green." You can hear Ella Fitzgerald sing it on the Nat King Cole TV show by going to YouTube.

Perhaps Mom's favorite song, though, was "Wayfaring Stranger," an old folk hymn in a minor key, in which the singer's yearning for something more than life has to offer is unmistakeable.

> *I'm just a poor, wayfaring stranger,*
> *a-traveling through this world of woe.*
> *Yet there's no sickness, toil nor danger*
> *In that bright land to which I go.*
> *I'm going there to see my mother.*
> *I'm going there no more to roam.*
> *I am just going over Jordan—*
> *I am just going over home.*

That one was always followed by another old hymn that began, "I will arise and go to Jesus./ He will embrace me in his arms./ In the arms of my dear savior, oh, there are ten thousand charms!" Her voice, a somewhat nasal alto, had a small range and no vibrato, but the suppressed emotion and longing in her delivery never failed to touch me.

Mother came by her musical talents naturally. Although I never heard him sing or play, Mom's father, James Harrison Rainbolt, had been a trumpet player and singer in his youth, before his struggle to support a growing family in the midst of the Great Depression apparently silenced the music in him forever. I've seen a picture of him with a band, but he was always just an observer when I was growing up and the family gathered around the piano on holidays. I suspect, though, that one of the songs we always sang when we got together came straight from him. I can't even find it on Google, so I'm going to write it in full here, the best I can remember:

> *Went down to Cuba when the war broke out,*
> *I took my razor and my gun.*
> *Went down to Cuba when the war broke out,*
> *I was dyin' to have some fun.*

War broke out in eighteen and one,
I had nothin' left but my gun.
Cannon ball flew over my head,
and this is what I said:
"Captain, captain, I wanna go home
I don't wanna fight.
B'lieve to my soul I got the heart disease,
I don't feel just right.
If I should die, so far away from home,
how the girls would weep and moan.
Write me a pension for the rest of my life,
and show me the way to go home."

That's the way I remember it, but I can't find any information about a war in Cuba in 1801, so it was probably a much later date, maybe 1901 in the Spanish-American War, which was triggered by the sinking of the Battleship Maine in Havana harbor on February 15, 1898. From that song, we would immediately segue into the better-known "Show me the way to go home,/ I'm tired and I wanna go to bed . . ."

Mama was the eldest of eight children, and all but the last two were extremely musical. The most talented were Aunt Bess and Uncle Jim, who could play any instrument you put in their hands if you gave them a little time to experiment. I have a photo of Mom when she was 17, sitting at the piano. Grouped around her are her sister Edith, 15, holding a harmonica; Jim, 10, banjo in hand; and Bess, 7, holding a child-sized violin. When she was in her 80s, I asked Aunt Bess when and how she had learned to play the violin. "I don't remember," she said. Her mind was as sharp as ever—she remembered Mama teaching her to play the piano—but music was so much a part of her that she had no idea when or how she had learned to play the violin. I don't know if she ever had formal lessons, but I do know she taught violin for awhile after she was grown. When she was 19, she went with a friend deep down in the Kentucky Mountains for a couple of years to be a missionary to the hill people, way back where there was no running water or electricity, and she took her accordion and violin. Later, she used to make us all laugh by singing and playing the accordion—the left hand playing in one key, the right in another, while she sang the melody in a third. She could also sing off-key on purpose, like Miss Worm on the old Captain Kangaroo show. If you don't think that's hard for a good singer to do, just ask one. When Mom and her two sisters sang trios, their voices blended like wine and water. Aunt Bess had a more classical-style voice and a range that would almost rival that of the famous Peruvian singer, Ima Sumac, going from tenor to soprano. Aunt Edith, only modestly talented but with a nice voice, always sang soprano in their trios and Mom sang alto, with Bess somewhere in between, above, or below, as she saw fit. Either Mom or Aunt Bess would accompany on the piano, and in some of the recordings I have, you can hear them trying out different keys to see which one would suit them best. Although they could read music, they rarely had to, since they could play any popular song or hymn by ear, in any key. Aunt Bess even played some classical pieces by ear, adding her own little touches.

Uncle Jim not only played guitar, organ, and banjo—and bass drum in the Shriners marching band—but he wrote poems and clever little lyrics that he set to music. I still think if his kids ever tried to sell his songs, they could make a mint. One of them, called "Peanuts," was a bouncy little ditty about President Jimmy Carter. Several were about how much Uncle Jim loved his children, although all five children, now that they are grown and he is dead, say he was terribly abusive to them when they were little. When I learned that, the bottom almost dropped out of my heart because he had always been my favorite uncle, awesomely talented in so many ways, and loads of fun. I shouldn't have been so shocked, though, since, to a lesser degree, my own mother was sometimes physically and emotionally abusive when I was growing up—something I'm sure she had learned from her father, who inflicted much more pain on her in her childhood than I ever suffered from her hands. Obviously, music doesn't always have sufficient power to soothe a savage breast, but it does seem to bind people together. Mom, who was the only child who could remember when her dad had made music, loved him in spite of his abuse. She told me that, when he was dying, he said to her, "I never thought you loved me," to which she replied, "You never let me."

As I was growing up, I taught myself to play some of Mom's songs, but the chord progressions in "Wayfaring Stranger" and "Dancing on the Ceiling" were too complicated for me. I can only pick out the melodies a note at a time. The reason I had to play songs by ear was that I never learned to read music very well. Mom's early efforts to teach me piano usually ended with her angry and me in tears, so she sent me to another woman in town for lessons. But after a couple of years of watching that woman's long, lacquered fingernails click over the keys, I was dismissed. "Come back when you're ready to practice," my teacher said. For years I thought the problem was my laziness and impatience: I could play most songs well enough by ear to amuse myself, and I hated having to start each piece over from the beginning every time I made a mistake, which was that teacher's method. After Mom died, though, Aunt Bess told me that Grandma had declared, "The reason Pat never learned to play the piano was that Mary Ruth [my mom] would never get off the bench." I suspect there was some truth to that. I was so awed by my mother's talent that I was afraid to compete. And competition, along with music and violence, was in my mother's genes.

Still, I learned a lot of music from her. I was singing harmony before first grade, and by the time I was in third or fourth grade, Mom had put me in a trio of little girls at the church where she and Dad were co-pastors. I sang the alto part. We often sang on my parents' radio program, which was broadcast from the now-defunct Broadview Hotel in East St. Louis, Illinois, every Sunday afternoon in the late 1940s and early '50s. When we entered our teens, our trio branched out to popular music, in the style of the Maguire Sisters, who had, in turn, styled themselves after the Andrew Sisters of the WW II era. We performed for a few local events—a fashion show is the only one I actually remember—and I like to think that if my partners had been as dedicated to the group as I was, we might have had a chance as professionals. But every time a boy asked one of them for a date, she would miss practice, and eventually we went our separate ways. The soprano of our group—a kind of poor man's Marilyn Monroe— was still trying to make it in Nashville, though, when she was in her forties, on her fourth marriage, and the mother of four kids. I still have a copy of her demo tape. She died in her 60s of alcohol-related problems, I heard.

From 5th through 9th grade, I also flirted with playing the flute, both solo and in the school band. The highlight of my flute period was a local concert in Collinsville, Illinois, in which I played "Tico Tico," a fast piece requiring considerable breath control and dexterity. During the applause, my dad stood up and whistled, and afterwards, my old piano teacher remarked kindly, "Well, Pat, you seem to be making much better progress on the flute!" I still wasn't big on practicing, though, and gave up playing by my junior year in high school. In 1989, I finally gave the instrument to the Lincoln High School Jazz Band in East St. Louis, which was so good it had been invited to play at the Montreux Jazz Festival in France. A lot of the band members were too poor to afford their own instruments, so I decided that my flute could finally be put to good use. Singing was always my first love, anyway.

My desire to be a singer met with some obstacles during my teens, though. My parents' church didn't believe in a lot of things, including wearing makeup, drinking, smoking, gambling, playing cards, going to movies and dancing. Even TV, which was in its infancy in my childhood, was still suspect among a lot of our members. I was shocked one time when I heard my mother declare to a church member that she had never been to the opera. They had been talking about the giant St. Louis "Muny" outdoor theater, which, in those days, still went by the name of the St. Louis Municipal Opera, and I knew for a fact that Mom had been to productions there because I had gone with her. When I called her on it after the parishioner left, Mom replied sternly, "Pat, the Municipal Opera is musical theater. I have never been to the opera." Case closed. Mom was an expert at misleading her hearers without technically telling a lie. If she hadn't chosen the ministry, she probably could have forged a successful career in law or politics.

I know Mom enjoyed going to the Muny, but when, as a teenager, I wanted to try out for the Muny chorus, she wouldn't let me. She was afraid some of our members would find out, and since our main source of income was the tithes and freewill offerings they put in the plate on Sundays, we couldn't afford to offend them. So, naturally, when I heard during my junior year of high school that KMOX radio was sponsoring a contest and auditioning performers at area high schools, I didn't dare tell her that I planned to try out. In those days, KMOX, the largest station in St. Louis and one of the most powerful in the midwest, had its own pianist, Lee Sanguinette, and a full orchestra, led by Stan Dougherty. Students who were chosen for the new show, called "Teen O'Clock Time," would get to sing or play with the orchestra in the Starlight Roof ballroom on the top floor of the Chase-Park Plaza hotel, the most elegant establishment of its kind in the St. Louis metropolitan area.

For two or three weeks before the auditions at our school, I went around secretly practicing "St. Louis Blues." Since I had heard my mother sing it all of my life, I knew it by heart. When the big day finally arrived, I didn't even have sheet music for the pianist. "Can you play 'St. Louis Blues' in the key of C?" I asked somewhat timidly. "Sure, Honey," Sanguinette replied, whereupon he began to play and I launched into the blues. A week later I was thrilled to find that I was one of six students selected to perform on the show. I heard through the grapevine that my high school choir director was rather upset about it, since some of her private vocal students hadn't made the cut.

Presented with a *fait accompli*, my mother couldn't bring herself to forbid me to participate in the show. She also couldn't bring herself to show up in the ballroom on the day of the performance—what would our parishioners think? But she and Dad, along with a preacher friend and his wife, listened to me on the radio. Afterwards, she told me proudly that I was the only singer who had stayed perfectly on pitch—high praise, since I had heard her fault Frank Sinatra's pitch on occasion when he was still an up-and-coming singer.

That Saturday afternoon on KMOX radio turned out to be the highlight of my singing career. I didn't win any prizes—I was actually rather stiff and self-conscious as a solo performer—but I will always remember that day with pleasure. Researching "Teen O'Clock Time" for this essay, I was surprised to find that the popular Hilltoppers quartet had also appeared on the show in 1954, but I'm sure they weren't contestants, since they were already famous for their recording of "P.S., I love you" and other big hits. It's fun to know, though, that I sang on the same show as some stars of my teen years.

Shortly after I turned 19, I married Harold Piety. My new husband liked music, too, although he didn't play any instrument but the record player. He loved the classical composers—especially Bach, Beethoven, and Brahms—and he had a nice tenor voice, for which he had received a few lessons from a professional. A sportswriter for the now-defunct *East St. Louis Journal* when we met, he was seven years older than I, a college graduate, and a veteran of four years in the Navy during the Korean Conflict. When we were dating, he would sing "Green Eyes" to me, because my eyes were green, or the love song from "Tales of Hoffman." While I thought his singing was romantic, I also thought he looked a little bit silly the way the sides of his nose flared and pressed in as he forced his voice up into the proper cavities for resonance, as he had been taught to do. I'm sure it was the correct way to sing, but it seemed stiff and unnatural to me. I don't think I told him so, although my memory may be selective. He *was* kind of stuffy. Once, after we were married, when he explained to someone that his taste in music trended toward "the older, the better," my little brother, John, added drily, "Yeah, he's crazy about the sound of two sticks on a log." That became a family joke.

Before I turned 24, I was already the mother of three little girls. But their childhood was not marinated in music, as mine had been. They heard their dad's classical recordings, of course, along with albums of children's music that we bought for them and an occasional bit of jazz from my small collection, but my husband wasn't religious and I was entertaining agnostic thoughts myself, so we attended church only when visiting my parents. By the time the youngest was in first grade, we had moved to Ohio, away from my Mom and her family, so the girls missed out on most of the songfests at my grandparents' house, as well. In Ohio, we eventually started attending a church for social reasons, but the music there seemed dry and boring—not like the lively choruses I had grown up with. Moreover, all the hymns seemed to be pitched for choir boys—way too high for my alto—so in church I started singing in a very soft falsetto, or an octave lower, or not at all.

Although our two older girls took piano lessons briefly and studied violin for a couple of years in grade school, they didn't pursue music, except as listeners. But Julia, my youngest, taught herself to sing "St. Louis Blues" in almost exactly the same style as her grandmother and I. When she was in fifth or sixth grade, she was chosen as a featured performer in a local entertainment group called "Peanut Butter and Jelly" which was styled after the popular "Micky Mouse Club" on TV. Actor Rob Lowe, who, among other things, played Sam Seaborn in the popular "West Wing" series many years later, was another one of the stars in that group, which went around town putting on shows for schools and community groups. One Christmas, they even produced a show for local TV.

In her teens, Julia started taking classical guitar lessons because she said she figured if she could master the classical guitar, she could play any other kind of music. But after a couple of years, she said she realized that one never actually "masters" classical guitar. She continued to play and sing in bars when she was in college, but in the end she decided that pursuing a career in show business was too risky, so she went to law school and now she's a partner in her firm. I'm proud of her accomplishments as a lawyer, but, to my disappointment, she put away her guitar and never plays it any more.

When the girls' father was 46 years old, he fell in love with a girl just slightly older than our eldest daughter, who was then 18. I had already been unfaithful, so I had no moral ground on which to stand. For at least six months, we carried on conversations behind closed doors about what we were going to do. He threatened to leave me by a certain date, then postponed it because of a scheduled family reunion. In the meantime, the children and our parents didn't have a clue. (My parents, who had divorced a few years earlier after 34 years of marriage, were in Illinois. Harold's father was in California and his mother had died when he was 12). For some reason—perhaps my hope that a trip for just the two of us would bring us back together—I persuaded Harold to take me on a road trip to New Orleans while my mother came to stay with the girls, who were all in their teens. Harold and I had agreed that we would separate immediately after our return, but we still hadn't told a soul. I don't remember too much about that trip except walking down the middle of the street to our hotel in the French Quarter after a Dixieland performance at Preservation Hall, wearing a loose, floor-length "hostess dress" my mother had made for me that was more appropriate for a housecoat, and singing the blues at the top of my lungs. People probably thought I was drunk, but I don't think I'd had anything to drink. I was just sad. My husband tagged along, not asking me to pipe down. I also sang on most of the drive home. Sometime during the drive, he told me I had a lovely voice.

Around the time we separated, I developed a painful tightness in my throat, around my adam's apple and under my ears—something like that feeling you have when you're trying not to cry. The doctor diagnosed it as "inflamed carotid arteries" and prescribed prednisone, although doctors I have told about it in later years have been skeptical. Such a condition without more serious complications sounds highly unlikely, they say. Eventually the pain went away, but my voice never was the same. Now when I try to sing, I can't hold a note and my voice often cracks. I try not to think about it.

I comfort myself by listening to the many recordings of the family singing and playing that Aunt Bess made for me on tape, most of which she transferred to CDs before she died at the age of 86. On those recordings I can hear my mom's whole family singing hymns together, like a formal church choir, and I can pick out every voice. There are solos by several members of the family, including Uncle Jim playing the guitar and singing the songs he wrote—some funny, some very poignant, in light of what I now know about him. One of my most treasured tapes is from one of the rare times—perhaps the only time— that my mother, my daughters and I all sang together during a holiday get-together after I was divorced. We sound pretty good singing some old rounds and harmonizing on "Amen" and "Down in the Valley." We also sound as if we're having a really good time. I like to play that tape when I'm traveling in the car, reliving times when we were all happy together. But the recording that still tugs at my heartstrings is my mother's rendition of "I will arise, and go to Jesus . . ."

During the last 14 years of my mother's life, after both of us had been divorced for a long time, I spent almost every weekend with her, taking her to dinner on Saturday night, after which we would return to her home or, later, her assisted living apartment, where we would play Scrabble until bedtime. In the morning, even though I was—and still am—an agnostic, I would take her to her church, but the congregation had shrunk to a handful of people—mostly old—and the singing was no longer as lively as I remembered it from my childhood.

When Mama was 89 years old, she suffered a stroke. She lay in the hospital for several days, not eating or talking, and the doctor said either I had to put her on a feeding tube or move her to a nursing home. I knew she wouldn't want a feeding tube because she had already made a living will, but she had also cautioned me many times when I was growing up, "Don't ever put me in a nursing home!" I still had a couple of years to work in order to collect my retirement, and I couldn't care for her myself, so I put her in a nursing home close to my job and my condo. The place was pretty nice, as nursing homes go, and to my total surprise, the staff there quickly brought Mom back to the land of the living. I visited her almost daily, often stopping at MacDonald's or Long John Silver's to pick up sandwiches and fries that we could eat during my lunch hour out on the second-story sunporch. The home had a couple of pianos, so in the evenings I would sometimes play the old songs for her that I knew by ear—hymns and choruses and a popular song or two. "I didn't know you could play the piano so well," she commented one day. And, indeed, I think I played better there than I had in years, and I know I haven't played that well since.

The stroke had caused Mom to get confused about a lot of things, which was kind of a blessing. Whenever she asked about the place where she was staying, I would tell her it was a place for people to recuperate when they had been ill, carefully avoiding the dreaded words, "nursing home." I sometimes suspected that she actually knew what it was, though, because one of the attendants told me she occasionally cried at night, and once when I was with her she suddenly seemed to realize where she was and cried as if her heart would break. Most of the time, though, she seemed in pretty good spirits. She asked me a lot of details about my work and home situation, and she seemed concerned that I lived alone. Once she surprised me by asking, "Do you have much intercourse?" "No, Mama, not much," I said, touched by her concern and amused that old age had relieved her of so many inhibitions. She frequently talked about "going home to Mama," and after awhile I gave up on telling her that her mother was long dead. "I don't think it's time to go to your mama's," I told her. "Well, when will it be time?" she asked me. "I think she'll let you know," I said, half believing it myself. Once, when I asked if she knew her age, she answered "70." When I told her her real age, along with mine and that of her son and grandchildren, she seemed genuinely surprised. Without a word, she walked over to the piano, sat down and started playing, "Fairy tales, can come true/ it can happen to you/ if you're young at heart . . . ."

Early on Saturday morning, April 19, 2003, the nursing home called to tell me my mother was failing. When I got there, I took her hand in mine and she grabbed hold without opening her eyes or speaking. After a little while, I crawled into bed with her and snuggled up close. Still without opening her eyes, she pulled the oxygen tube out of her nose, but I put it back. When she pulled it out the second time, I said, "OK, Mama, if you don't want it, you don't have to have it." I don't know if she heard me, but while I was lying there holding her, I apologized tearfully for all the times I had hurt her, and I told her how much I loved her. "You're going home to mama," I assured her.

Looking back, I still find it hard to believe that I went to sleep as my mother was dying, but I did. I was awakened sometime later when a friend entered the room, and I discovered that Mom was breathing slowly and calmly, as if asleep. Without getting out of bed, I talked quietly for a couple of minutes with my friend, who had once been a novitiate in a convent, and, on impulse, I asked her to place her hand on Mother's forehead and say a prayer. A few minutes after my friend left, Mom gave one big shudder and it was all over.

I don't know whether she went home to her mama or was at last embraced in the arms of the Jesus she had always sung about—or maybe she finally found the lover who, all those years ago, had danced on the ceiling in her dreams. Perhaps she was just folded back into the great Mystery that is life. In any case, I know she left peacefully, and I'd like to think that her spirit was singing and confident of her destination.

My Mother's Piano

Mother's piano has sat idle for a couple of months or more.
I see it from the corner of my eye as I pass from room to room,
taunting me with memories, reminding me of old melodies
perhaps better left unsung.

Black box, sinister box, recorder of loves' worst disasters,
you bulge with blues and swooning ballads,
bad influences of my impressionable youth.

Pandora's box of family secrets, your keys unlock genealogies
of piano teachers and piano players
and family songfests of Christmases long past.

Stoic, silent music box, your strings resonate on the throbbing air,
constantly beseeching me, silently beguiling me
to lift your lid and touch your keys
and let our symphony out.

The Game

Note: This story is obviously fiction, since it is told from the husband's point of view. Moreover, as my mother said when I read it to her many years ago, "I never made dumplings in my life."

Paul laid a damp linen towel over the mound of bread dough and set the big clay bowl in a corner by the stove, where it would be free from drafts. Within an hour or so, the dough would rise to the top and he would have to come back and punch it down again. But in the meantime, they could begin the game.

Laura, who had been sitting at the kitchen table reading, looked up the moment he set the bowl down. "Ready?" she asked. Her brown eyes betrayed a momentary flicker of fear that tonight he would say no.

And, if the truth were known, he wasn't really ready. He would have liked to take a book into the living room and read in his favorite chair by the fire, or stretch out on the floor with his dog beside him, letting the glorious strains of Beethoven's "Pastorale" smooth over the day's ragged thoughts.

But he was unwilling to face Laura's frustration and disappointment if he said no—and even more unwilling to risk the likely after-effects in their bed later on. So, drying his hands on the kitchen towel as he removed it from around his waist, and affecting a hearty manner, he replied, "Ready! Let's play ping-pong!"

In December, when Laura had received her master's degree, she had informed him that a ping-pong table—something she had wanted since childhood—would be a most welcome graduation present, and

46

he had been happy to oblige. He was genuinely proud of the way she had persevered to earn her bachelor's degree and then her master's while raising their three children and teaching third grade. In fact, he had been surprised to find himself getting a bit choked up at the graduation ceremonies.

Now, though, he sometimes wished he had bought her something more traditional, like jewelry. These ping-pong matches were becoming a nightly ritual in which the "few games" stretched out to 10 or 15, or even more, as Laura, sweat soaking her T-shirt, entreated him for "one more game."

So far, she hadn't won a single game.

They descended the rickety steps to the dimly lit basement in silence and took their places at each end of the table. After a few games, they would switch sides.

As the long fluorescent fixture Paul had installed over the table cast its cool glow over Laura's face, he thought once again how attractive she still was after nearly 15 years of marriage. She was one of those women who had looked 25 at the age of 20 and now, at 32, with three children, she still looked 25. She would age well, he thought, like her mother.

A man, Paul was fond of saying, should choose the mother of his children in much the same way that he would choose a fine horse for breeding: good bones and teeth, strong constitution, and wide hips suitable for childbearing. Upon meeting Laura, he had almost immediately recognized that she fit the bill.

They had met at a campus lecture series, where Laura's healthy good looks and her bold questioning of the famous speaker had caught Paul's attention, so on the pretext that he wanted to discuss a point she had made, he invited her out for coffee. They were married just five months later.

Having finished a hitch in the Navy and received his degree on the G.I. Bill, Paul was ready to settle down and start a family. They agreed that Laura could go back to college part-time while the children were small, and perhaps even go full-time after they started to school, which is what she had done. Although Paul didn't place a lot of faith in the grades college professors handed out, he had to admit that Laura's transcript supported his own view that she was a highly intelligent woman—an important thing in a wife and mother.

It was important, too, that a mother be relatively free of neuroses, and on this point Paul often thought his judgment had been less than perfect. Although Laura had seemed well-balanced enough when they met—given her upbringing by fundamentalist preachers, which was admittedly a handicap—after the children were born she had developed a rather steady stream of minor physical ailments that seemed to be more imagined than real, and she was given to occasional crying jags and fits of moodiness.

He sometimes thought he would have sacrificed some of her intelligence for a more placid disposition, had he known what to expect. But for all he knew, maybe most women cried at night once a month or so. It could be the nature of the female sex. His intimate experiences with women before marriage had, admittedly, been limited to whores in the Navy and a couple of short-lived romances.

Paul had his own emotional quirks—he'd be the first to admit it—but if something was bothering him, he tended to keep it to himself. There was no point in burdening other people.

"Want to warm up a bit?" Paul asked what had become the traditional question.

"OK," Laura responded, dropping the ball over the net without further comment.

During these games, he mused as the volley got underway, Laura was uncharacteristically silent. Most of the time, unless she was annoyed with him for something, she could talk enough for both of them. At parties, Paul was usually the more verbal one, especially when someone got him started on the proper way to bake a loaf of bread or explaining why the Social Security system was a vast, chain-letter hoax that would lead to the ultimate destruction of the U.S. economy. On these occasions, he tended to forget about Laura's half-teasing comments about his "pontificating," he was so engrossed in the intricacies of his subject. But when they were alone, Laura did most of the talking, and he found the sound of her voice rather pleasant, even when he didn't pay much attention to what she was saying.

It seemed to Paul that he had never known anyone who could see the same topic from so many angles as Laura could. She walked around a subject in her mind, climbed on top of it, crawled under it, and peered around corners in her attempts to find a rational explanation for every experience in her life, although every time she examined one, she saw it in a different light, so that she was continually revising her opinions.

Paul was much more inclined to stick to the facts, and every once in awhile he felt compelled to remind her that her latest theory contradicted her previous one. Far from benefitting from his insight, though, she usually took the attitude that he didn't understand what she was trying to say, which was preposterous. He probably should just leave her to her mental exercises, but he couldn't resist the impulse to set her straight when she wandered too far afield.

Tonight's volley, he reflected, was lasting longer than usual—as a matter of fact, they had been getting steadily longer—but he knew that the odds were still heavily in his favor. He wasn't a great player by any means—he had met several men in the Navy who could polish him off in minutes—but he had a fair degree of athletic ability and more experience with the game than Laura, not to mention the fact that she was a bit awkward and unsure of herself at sports. All he had to do most of the time was return the ball until she missed. Once in awhile— and the times were becoming more frequent, he had to admit—he yielded to the urge to put a little spin on his serves. When she lofted a ringer over to him, only a saint could resist slamming it. And Paul was no saint. Laura never complained when she lost the point, though. Ignoring the indulgent chuckle he sometimes allowed himself, she simply served again or tossed the ball back with a terse "your serve." But he could tell that it got to her.

For a brief period, she had actually teased him rather mercilessly when he missed a shot, and he had to admit that it had rattled him just a bit, but she had quit doing that almost as quickly as she had started it. Trash-talking was definitely a male practice. Women just weren't that good at it, which is probably why she had stopped.

But even though she hadn't won a game yet, all that practice was starting to pay off. Laura was getting to be a pretty fair defensive player. Her problem, though, was that, all things being equal, a good offense could beat a good defense nine times out of ten.

Paul won the volley, as usual, starting the game off with a slicing serve to the far left corner which, to his surprise, Laura returned with apparent ease. As the play continued, he noticed that her backhand had improved considerably since those first games, only now she tended to hit everything backhanded.

That was typical of Laura. She seemed to find it hard to achieve any sort of balance, in life as well as in ping-pong. She had a tendency to go off the deep end with her enthusiasms, and her reaction to criticism was inclined to be exaggerated. "Laura's apocalyptic view of the universe," Paul had labeled it. As he had told her more than once, she had an almost crippling insecurity. An insult from any old bum in the gutter could throw her into an agony of self-doubt. But other people's criticism was nothing to what she could put her own self through at times.

This tendency to overreact and take things personally made it hard for her to take advice, at least from Paul. Any benefit superior age or experience he ventured to proffer—from how to make lump-free mashed potatoes to how to put spin on her serve—was apt to be received with undue defensiveness. He had stopped trying to teach her anything about sports, but when it came to subjects like how to make hospital corners on the bedsheets or how to create light, airy dumplings, rather than the heavy, gummy type Laura's mother still made, he felt it was well within reason for him to offer helpful hints. After all, he had to sleep in the bed and eat the food, too, and it would be downright perverse to live with mediocre quality in these things when a remedy was so easily at hand.

Paul's thoughts came quickly back to the game when Laura gave him a taste of his own medicine with a serve that barely shaved the edge of the table and dropped like a rock.

"A lucky shot," he grinned, retrieving the ball from a dusty corner under the laundry tubs.

"I seem to notice that the harder I try, the luckier I get," she countered. "Whoever said that first knew what he was talking about."

Paul had no trouble conceding that Laura had come a long way. What she didn't know, though, was how far she had to go. That fact often created an uncomfortable situation for him. If he made a game too easy, she accused him of not really trying, and she was insulted and frustrated. But if he pulled out all the stops and played as he would against a true peer, she would set her jaw in a grim way that he had come to recognize as a signal that the evening would be long on play and short on friendly conversation.

It wasn't fair, damn it! Maybe men and women would be better off if they limited their mutual participation in sports to dancing and making love.

While he had been wool-gathering, Paul suddenly became aware that Laura had been gaining on him. The score was tied up: twenty all. He had little doubt that he could win, but maybe it wouldn't hurt to pull his punches ever so slightly and let her have this one. She had been waiting for it for a long time, and maybe a win for her would give him a bit of relief from these nightly contests.

It had become their custom after the evening's play to share a small loaf of bread fresh from the oven, slathered with butter and washed down with steaming cups of black coffee. If the play had not gone too badly, these late-night tete-a-tetes in their little breakfast room at the back of the house could be very cozy indeed. Laura's unabashed enthusiasm for the simple act of eating, like her love of conversation, was among the traits that had attracted him to her in the days of their courtship. Sharing a warm loaf of bread on a cold winter night could be a pleasant after-game experience, which, with a little luck, could lead to an even more pleasant experience in bed.

In the instant that he sent the ball flying back over the net, the quite unexpected thought flashed through Paul's mind that, looking back on these ping-pong nights in years to come, he might actually miss them.

Apprenticeship

For Harold

I wanted you to be all my variety.
While I sat quietly spinning,
I sent you in search of winning
hard battles and fighting
fierce dragons that were—
alas—never my own.

Thus the tapestry I wove,
though rich and shot with gold,
was yours alone to treasure,
for the boundaries of warp and woof
and the fabric's unique design
were made to your measure—
not mine.

Now, working here on my own,
I choose a fresh shuttle to hold
the thread of my hopes
and find heaps of yarn in tangles—
mine and yours, wrapped up altogether,
like yesterday's dreams, intertwined.

So this new cloth I'm learning to weave,
though my own, is not only mine.
While its slowly emerging pattern and
yours cannot be the same,
it bears a lingering aura of the spinning
I did in your name.

Houses

I dream a lot about houses. In the most common dream, I live in a house that is three stories tall. The third story, although furnished, is largely unused. But knowing it's there gives me a delicious feeling of expansiveness—of room to spare. I'm still trying to figure out what the dream means, although I have some ideas.

Over the past 74 years, I've lived in six states, in virtually every kind of housing but a trailer—new houses, old ones, apartments, a condo, and a dormitory. Still, like past lovers, certain houses hold a special place in my memory.

The first of these could be called "The House That Mom Built." In the early 1940s, my parents went on the road as Pentecostal evangelists, taking me with them. During those years before I started to school, we lived in hotels and other peoples' homes. I loved the life and could have happily gone on traveling forever, but after awhile, Mom apparently got a hankering for a place of her own, so she asked her mother to go with her to the Savings and Loan in Collinsville, Illinois, where her parents lived, to ask for a loan. When the director learned she had only $10 to her name and no regular income, he told her sadly that he couldn't in good conscience give her a loan. And that's when Mom cried. She wasn't usually the crying type, but I guess being so long without a place to call home had got to her.

"Well," the director said, weakening, "Your dad's a good customer of ours and a good carpenter. Since he's giving you a piece of land, I guess we could advance you a little money to get started."

So with instructions from her 20-year-old brother Jim and help from brother Bob, 17, Mom dug the footings and they managed to erect a little house with a kitchen, living room, bedroom and tiny bath, furnished with fixtures Grandpa had salvaged from buildings he had helped to tear down down in his job as foreman for a construction company. Grandpa's friend, Mr. Dallas Hicks, built the kitchen cabinets, which Mom painted white and decorated with flower decals. We lived in that house off and on for about 10 years.

Originally, the heat came from an isinglass-windowed stove in the living room, where I slept on a fold-out davenport. Once, in the middle of winter, I got mad about something and threw a nickel in the fire. When my mother realized what I'd done, she gave me a spanking. Covered in thick woolen overalls against the winter cold, I hardly felt her blows. "Hmph—that didn't hurt," I informed her with satisfaction, whereupon she promptly removed my leggings and administered the punishment all over again—this time to greater effect.

At first, water had to be heated on the stove, so we used it sparingly. Every Monday, we would remove the bedsheets, putting the bottom sheet in the wash and transferring the top sheet to the bottom (fitted sheets hadn't been invented yet). To keep the sheets as clean as possible, we also bathed in the evening, before bedtime, and because hot water was in short supply, we sometimes shared bathwater, adding more from the teakettle as the water cooled down.

An icebox in the kitchen kept our food cold. Every few days, we would put a big white card in the window: If the "25" was at the top, the iceman brought a 25-pound block of ice. By turning the card upside down, we could order 50 pounds.

The milk truck, loaded with crates packed in ice, came down our street every day to deliver full bottles and to pick up empty ones. One of my chief delights was getting the milkman to give me some ice chips to crunch on. I also chewed on pieces of tar the paving truck laid down on the street once a summer, oblivious to the potential hazard to my health.

The bakery truck came a couple of times a week, honking the horn to draw neighbors out to the street, whereupon the driver would open his back doors and display trays of tempting goodies. Well-known for my love of cheesecake, I was often the lucky recipient of a slice bought for me by one of the neighbor ladies, whose kitchens I haunted when time weighed heavily on my hands.

By the time I was in third grade, members of the church my parents were now pastoring had helped dig out a basement under the house to install a coal-burning furnace. We also bought a Frigidaire for the kitchen. While Dad was away one summer, mom had her two brothers build a garage a few feet from the house, and when he returned, he and the neighbors built a "breezeway" connecting the garage to the kitchen. I can still picture my parents and the neighbors standing on either side of the porch, smoothing out the concrete with a 2x4. Soon Mama acquired a wringer washer and the breezeway became our laundry room, so we didn't have to go to Grandma's on laundry day any more. The stairs to the basement ran alongside the breezeway, and sewage from the sink, kitchen and laundry went to a "cesspool" in the yard, which Daddy dug and lined with bricks before we got a modern septic tank.

When I was almost nine, my brother was born and a large dormer was added to the attic to accommodate a second bedroom. And when I was in sixth grade, a whole wing was added, with two bedrooms and a bath upstairs and a living room and library for all Dad's books downstairs. (In addition to being a preacher, he dealt in rare books by mail and loved to read, so our house was always full of books.) Twice when we added on to the house, Daddy had to transplant my favorite weeping willow because it was in the way of progress.

That house had a lot of neat nooks and crannies. Because the basement had been dug out after the house was built, it had an earthen shelf a couple of feet wide extending inward from the footings, which was dark and climatically perfect in winter for storing potatoes and other produce from my dad's abundant garden.

The upstairs hallway between the new wing and the dormer bedroom had a little ramp where Uncle Jim had miscalculated floor heights between the old part and the new. When my parents were away, I loved roller-skating up and down that ramp. Running short of wallpaper, Dad had covered a space in the hall next to the stairs with pictures of fashions from *Godey's Lady Book*. I spent lots of time admiring those women with their satin bustles, fancy parasols, big hats and Gibson Girl hairdos.

Behind the clothes rack in my parents' bedroom was a windowless storage area extending into the new wing. If you didn't know it was there, you would never find it, which made it a perfect place for escaping from chores, quietly reading a book, or playing pretend with friends in winter.

Today, when I'm stressed out, I find it soothing to lie in bed and go over every inch of that house in my memory.

*   *   *

Fast forward 20 years or so to the fall of 1969, when my eldest daughter was in sixth grade, the middle one in third and the youngest in first. After serving as press secretary for the late Sen. Paul Simon's successful campaign for lieutenant governor of Illinois, their father had accepted a job as a feature writer for the *Dayton Journal Herald* in Ohio. I had just begun graduate school on a much-coveted scholarship to Washington University in St. Louis, so had I been consulted about his decision, we probably never would have moved to Ohio. But after one semester of commuting from Illinois to Wash U while taking care of a house and three children with only a part-time babysitter for help, I threw in the towel and joined him.

"Where else but Dayton View?" asked the ad touting the lovely inner-city neighborhood with its racially integrated homeowners. Lured by the brochure, we began our search there—and found the house of our dreams: a 50-year-old two-story white frame with a front porch, spacious attic, basement, detached garage and terraced back yard. As soon as we saw it, we all agreed that it had to be ours. The owner, an eccentric, middle-aged Jewish bachelor, must have been moved by our enthusiasm because he let us buy it "contract-for-deed," since we didn't have enough cash for a downpayment, even though the price was far below what the same house would have brought in the all-white suburbs.

That house had two gas fireplaces—one in the living room, which we later converted to wood-burning, and a tiny one in the master bedroom, which stretched from the front to the back of the house, affording a delightful cross draft that made air conditioning largely

unnecessary in Ohio's moderate climate. A full staircase to the attic ran right outside our bedroom door. Although Harold and I prided ourselves on being rational, un-superstitious sorts, we both thought we heard someone walking up the stairs late one night when we were in bed. If so, it must have been a friendly ghost because it didn't scare us away.

That attic stairway had a landing with a cozy window seat overlooking the back yard. Rustic wooden panels covered the two long walls, so finishing it was an easy job. The carpet we installed was deep red, and the black-and-white wallpaper at each end of the room, with its drawings of Victorian women, reminded me of the *Godey's Lady Book* pictures in The House That Mom Built. Being a chronic worry wart, I also had Harold nail a tall aluminum ladder outside one window, in case of fire. With the installation of a wall air conditioner, the attic renovation was complete, and we informed the girls that they could take turns living up there, a year at a time.

However, Titi, our middle daughter, was so entranced by her private hideaway that removing her from it became a challenge Harold and I were reluctant to take on. During her first winter in that room, Titi read books and watched TV documentaries and the "700 Club" for hours on end, rarely coming down except for meals or to go to school.

After a couple of years, though, she came home one day to find that all her belongings had been moved down to her younger sister's bedroom. Julie, fed up with waiting, had taken matters into her own hands and moved Titi's stuff to the attic.

When Julie was a teenager, I made the terrifying discovery that she had been sneaking out the window in the middle of the night to climb down the ladder and roam the neighborhood with her friends. The distance from the third floor to the ground looked frightening; moreover, although Dayton View was a beautiful and friendly neighborhood, it was sometimes dangerous in the racially turbulent 1979s. After that, I never slept well again, thinking every creak in the night could mean that Julie was climbing down the ladder. But she survived, as most teenagers do.

Tammy, the oldest, didn't seem to be in a hurry to move, perhaps because we had installed a ballet barre and a full-length mirror in her room. When she wasn't taking ballet lessons or dancing onstage, she was reading historical novels about European royalty, so she was somewhat indifferent to earthly dwellings.

(Side note: After they were grown, Tammy and Julie, who became a law professor and an attorney respectively, insisted on being addressed by their given names, "Tamara" and "Julia," but Marilyn, although she became the much-published Ph.D. philosopher M.G. Piety, still to this day asks her family to call her Titi—short for "Tiger.")

In the spring, the terraced back yard at our house in Dayton View was a Technicolor wonder, with its two cherry trees, three apple trees, and hoards of dandelions and wild violets, all in bloom. Harold Piety wasn't what you would call a dedicated lawn man, but he made up for that by growing raspberries and strawberries, which we all enjoyed fresh from the garden on cereal as well as in his homemade pies and jams.

In addition to being a gardener and jelly maker, Harold was also a bread baker of note. After I received my master's degree in English from the University of Dayton, he bought me a ping-pong table as a graduation present, something I had wanted since childhood, and we played many games in the basement while the bread dough was rising next to the old gravity furnace. Those ping-pong games became a kind of metaphor for our marriage: I quickly learned that I was no match for Harold, a natural athlete, but my competitive nature wouldn't let me concede defeat, so I insisted on playing game after game until the sweat poured off me. It can't have been much fun for Harold, but late at night after the games were over, we enjoyed sharing a cup of coffee and thick, warm slices of Harold's bread, slathered with butter, in the little breakfast room off the kitchen. After a few months and hundreds of games, I was able to win often enough to restore my self-esteem, so Harold could go back to reading or lying on the living room floor, his dog beside him, listening to Beethoven.

*   *   *

The only constant in life is change, someone said, and that was certainly true of our little paradise in Dayton View. By 1978, Harold and I had divorced, Tamara was attending community college and living with a Persian boyfriend, Titi was still living with her father in the house and attending her senior year at Colonel White High School in Dayton View, and Julia had moved with me to an apartment in Kettering, Ohio, where she was a sophomore at the public high school. The years between my divorce in 1978 and 2003, when I retired from a career as an underpaid publications editor and ghostwriter for institutional executives, are the subject of another essay on a wholly different life.

*   *   *

During the last 14 years before my retirement from full-time work, I lived in St. Louis and spent almost every weekend with my mother, who was living alone in Belleville, Illinois. After finishing my housekeeping chores on Saturday, I would drive across the Mississippi to take her to dinner, then go to her place to play Scrabble and spend the night, often taking her to church on Sunday morning and to lunch afterwards. Like me, Mom moved around a lot, so during those years she lived in a house, an apartment, the same house again, a senior living facility run by nuns in an old hotel, and an assisted living apartment, all in Illinois.

In the meantime, I was living in a high-rise condo in St. Louis' Central West End. A delightful neighborhood full of sidewalk cafes, art galleries, and the sumptuous Chase-Park Plaza hotel, the Central West End also contained lovely tree-lined, gated side streets with elegant three-story homes from the late 19th and early 20th centuries, each one more beautiful than the next. In the fall and spring, I especially liked to walk down these streets, admiring the homes and thinking how nice it would be if, after retirement, I could get together with some congenial friends to purchase one of them, so that we could each have our private quarters but share some common living areas. I knew, realistically, that it would never happen, though; I simply didn't have enough money—or know enough friends who were able to buy into the idea or would want to. Still, it was a pleasant fantasy.

Less than two years before I retired, I was forced to put Mom in a nursing home in St. Louis, two places she had always vowed she never wanted to live. I hated to do it, but I still had to work to be eligible for a pension, and my job and my condo were in St. Louis, so when the doctor said my choice was to have a feeding tube installed in her or move her out of the hospital, I opted to bring her closer to me. She had already signed a living will and I knew she didn't want a feeding tube. When I moved her, I fully expected that she would die within the next few days. She had stopped eating and was unresponsive when we tried to talk to her; it seemed that she had made up her mind to die. When I took her to the home that night, a young attendant started preparing her for bed. "We'll have her up and around tomorrow," she said. "You don't realize how far gone she is," I thought. But when I came back to the nursing home on my lunch hour the next day, I found Mom sitting in a wheel chair. "Is that Pat?" she said brightly. "I'm so glad to see you!" Eventually, she even got well enough to go out to Steak 'n Shake with me for dinner on Saturday nights whenever I felt up to lugging her wheelchair in the trunk of my car.

Mom's move to the nursing home, Beauvais Manor on the Park, had been so sudden and so unplanned that I didn't get to see all of the facility before I installed her in it, so I was astounded when I discovered that it was attached to a bona fide historical mansion from the the Civil War period. Constructed in 1864 for silversmith Renee Beauvais, the Greek-Revival structure across from the graceful Victorian-style Tower Grove Park had been converted into a home for elderly Protestant women in 1882. When it became a nursing home/rehabilitation center in 1983, a modern wing was added, but sometime during those years the mansion part had been restored to its original beauty, complete with period furnishings and clothing draped across the canopied bed and hanging in the closets. While Mom was living there, the mansion could be rented out for club meetings and special events, but when not in use, it was accessible to residents of the nursing home by means of indoor ramps. Residents could even reserve the sumptuous dining room for celebrations of their own, such as the 90th birthday party I hosted for my mother there.

Pushing my mother's wheelchair from the nursing home to the mansion in Beauvais Manor always seemed to me like going through the Looking Glass into Wonderland. I could never quite believe it was real. As the result of several small strokes, Mama was pretty fuzzy on details and I did what I could to keep her from realizing that she was in a nursing home—and in St. Louis, instead of her beloved Illinois. As we explored those beautiful rooms together, I would say, "See, Mama, you always wanted to live in a mansion, and now you do!"

*   *   *

Still, I cherished the hope that I would be able to move Mom out of Beauvais Manor and in with me before she died, so during the last year before I retired, I started making plans to move to Oklahoma, where I would be nearer to Tamara, who was now a law professor at University of Tulsa; Julia, who had become a partner in a law firm in Enid; and my brother John, who was a copy editor for the *Dallas Morning News.*

Through the Internet and a couple of site visits, I found the perfect place: a 100-year-old farmhouse in the middle of Stillwater, Oklahoma, with three porches, a porch swing, and a huge yard with 80-ft. trees and tall, flowering crape myrtle bushes. I pictured Mama sitting in her wheelchair on the side porch, looking out over the wide lawn and listening to the chimes from the Oklahoma State University library that I had enjoyed so much during my year as a freshman there, half a century before. We would have dinners with my children, I thought, and John and his family could come up for visits. Between trips to Oklahoma to finalize the sale, I told Mama about the house and how we were going to live there together. I wasn't sure she understood, but one of the nurses told me she had said we were going to move, so I thought she had at least a vague idea of what I was planning.

While driving down to Stillwater to sign the papers for the house, I received a call on my cell phone from one of the nurses at Beauvais Manor. "I hear you've asked the doctor to give your mother something to improve her appetite," she said. When I admitted having done so, she told me, "You need to understand that your mother is not dying because she's not eating; she's not eating because she's dying." Although it was sad news, I have always been grateful for her words, because it helped to relieve some of the guilt I felt about letting my mother go. Nevertheless, I hoped to get her to Oklahoma in time to die at home, so the nurse and I chatted for awhile about ways to transport her there, since she was too weak to travel as a regular passenger in the car and the cost of an ambulance would be prohibitive. I was considering renting a van and hiring someone to ride with her in the back, where she could lie down. The nurse agreed that my idea might work.

On my way home from Stillwater, I stopped by Beauvais Manor. "Mama, I bought the house," I told her. "You did?" she said. "Good." The note of "mission accomplished" in her voice was unmistakable. She died in my arms a few days later. I've always thought she felt she could leave me, now that I had a home of my own near my family.

*   *   *

Mama died on April 19, 2003, and in May of that same year, I retired from my job as Director of Development, Alumni Affairs and External Publications at Harris-Stowe State College (a big title with a considerably smaller salary attached) and moved to the little house in Stillwater. At last—a home of my own! The condo in St. Louis had been pleasant and modern, with a balcony and swimming pool—and even a doorman—but this was a *house*, and it was all mine! For several years, I had imagined scenarios in which I might become homeless, since I had spent the retirement money from several of my previous jobs in advance, taking each of my daughters to Europe after high school graduation; visiting my mother in Paraguay, where she had taught for a couple of years after her retirement; and going to see Titi in Denmark, to which she had originally traveled on a Fulbright Fellowship but where she remained for eight years. I had also traveled extensively in the U.S. and Mexico, as well as parts of Canada. My philosophy was that I wanted to spend what money I had while I was still able to enjoy it and hope I would die of a sudden heart attack or get hit by a truck before senility set in. In preparation for a half-anticipated life of penury, I had even scoped out public places to sleep, take baths and get around when I was no longer working. The only thing I hadn't figured out to my satisfaction was how to get nutritious meals without a refrigerator or stove. My daughter Tamara used to tease me that I was the only person she knew whose retirement plan was to be a bag lady. So I could hardly believe that I was actually a homeowner after retirement.

The floors in the old house slanted so badly that I had to put some of the furniture diagonally in corners to disguise the slope, and when I pounded nails in the walls to hang pictures, I could hear the rotting plaster crumbling down behind the thick textured vinyl wallpaper the previous owner had pasted over it to disguise its flaws. But it was my house, and it was charming. The double-lot yard—130 ft. x150 ft.—was like my own little park in the middle of a town that had grown around it. A long porch, complete with porch swing, swept across the entire east side, from which I could sit and look out toward a magnificent old cedar tree perhaps as old as the house. To my left were several large, blossom-covered magnolias, so densely packed that I discovered only later they were not one single tree. A climbing red rose clung to the white picket fence and large white roses rose up to the gutters in back. An old iron pump (no longer working but great for atmosphere) stood by the back door. I was in heaven.

The previous owner had converted the attic into two tiny rooms and a three-quarter bath with shower. When my daughter Julia went with me to inspect the house before I bought it, she said, "I don't think you could even get a bed into one of these rooms." But I did. The L-shaped room with its steeply slanted ceiling had just enough space in its fatter leg to accommodate a double bed. Lying in that bed, I could gaze out the diamond-shaped window in the dormer at the purple blossoms on the crape myrtle that reached up over the eaves. Under downy covers in wintertime, I felt a delicious coziness in that room. The other upstairs room, long and narrow, I turned into a study where I spent hours writing and playing Scrabble and Spider Solitaire on the computer.

I felt so settled in that house that I ventured to acquire two cats from the farm outside town where daughter Julia's sister-in-law lived. Daisy, the black-and-white female, roamed the yard by day, following me as I raked leaves and pruned plants, or sitting with me on the park bench under the big oak tree. Sometimes she would even join me on the porch swing. Felix, the all-black male, had allergies, so he had to stay inside. But both cats loved dashing around the house and up and down the stairs or sitting on perches in the dormer windows to watch the mocking birds and cardinals that fluttered around outside.

Whenever I worked in the yard—and there was always plenty of work to do—I rediscovered a feeling of timelessness that I hadn't experienced since childhood: no past, no future, only the endless Now.

But time continues to flow on, no matter how hard we may try to slow it down. After five years, I began to realize that my beloved little house would eventually bankrupt me, both financially and physically. Although I mowed my own lawn and trimmed the bushes myself, several times a year I had to hire someone to haul off all the fallen and trimmed branches. One January, in the midst of a dangerous drought, I raked and filled 80 large lawn bags with leaves in two weeks, trying to protect my house from fire. Trees died and had to be cut down. One tree service wanted $5,000 to trim the taller trees and cut down the sick or dying ones. The roof on the laundry room had to be repaired, and the floor had to be replaced. I had already poured thousands of dollars into buying appliances, having cabinets built and making other improvements, and my small savings account was rapidly getting smaller. Then the termites attacked the posts holding up the roof over the front porch. Long mocked by family members for my "apocalyptic view of the universe," I went into full panic mode, imagining the house falling down around me, even after the termite man had fixed the damage and installed an expensive protection system.

I loved my little house more than anything I had ever owned in life, but I was tired and scared. Moreover, I was lonely for St. Louis. The people of Stillwater had been incredibly kind to me, but I missed the stimulation of city life. I had grown up across the river from St. Louis and many of my most pleasant memories were associated with that city, going shopping or to the zoo or attending musical theatre in the magnificent outdoor "Muny" theatre. I had never actually lived in St. Louis until the age of 50, when I moved there from Phoenix to be nearer to my aging parents, but I ended up living there 14 years—longer than anywhere else in my life—before I moved to Oklahoma. So St. Louis, I finally realized, was truly my home town. My daughters were very busy with their careers and I didn't get to see them as often as I had imagined I would, and my brother, a victim of the declining fortunes of daily newspapers, had lost his job in Dallas and was now working for the *St. Petersburg Times*, in Florida. So in 2009, I reluctantly sold the house in Stillwater and returned "home."

It wasn't easy. I still grieve for my little house. And although I found a charming apartment across the street from the Missouri Botanical Garden, that wasn't destined to last, either. I had been feeling sick throughout the summer of 2011, and one night, about 2 a.m., the ceiling over my bathtub suddenly caved in, bringing with it a mass of dark, ugly "stuff." Fearing black mold, I hastily put Daisy in her carrier (Felix, frightened by the noise, was hiding out and had to be picked up later) and headed out in my car, wondering if I would, at last, be homeless, as I had so often feared.

*   *   *

Remember when I lived in the condo in the Central West End and used to walk down the gated streets fantasizing about buying one of the

large, three-storied houses with a group of congenial friends? Well, Dear Reader, life really is stranger than fiction sometimes. In the days that I was homeless after the collapse of my bathroom ceiling, Pam, a friend-of-a-friend who lives in one of those houses, took me in. An unrepentant, still un-yuppified hippie from the 1970s, she had bought the house in 1974, when most of the affluent whites were fleeing the city, for the incredible sum of $7,000. It's a gracious three-story brick with four fireplaces, and she now pays almost as much in annual property taxes as she originally paid for the whole house. The house where T.S. Eliot grew up is three blocks down the street, and a condo building half a block away bears a sign saying it was Tennessee Williams' childhood home (full disclosure: I've heard he didn't like St. Louis). And although Pam's house sits on a quiet, tree-lined street, it's only half a block from the shops, restaurants and galleries of the most coveted neighborhood in the city. The first Unitarian Church of St. Louis, of which I have been a member off and on since the 1960s, re-joining every time I returned to the metropolitan area, is two blocks away. It was founded by William Greenleaf Eliot, grandfather of T. S. and founder of Washington University.

When I first moved in with Pam, I intended to stay only long enough to find another apartment. After a disappointing search for something I could afford and still enjoy, she suggested that I might want to live in her house more permanently. "Remember how you said you had hoped to stay in your last apartment until you moved to the nursing home? Maybe you could just consider living here as a transitional phase," she said. It wasn't the most diplomatic way to phrase her proposal, I thought, but the more I considered it, the better it sounded.

My "quarters" consist of one large room stretching across the front of the house; it used to be two rooms and a hallway that have recently been combined and remodeled. There's a wood-burning fireplace at one end and a window seat at the other, with two large front-facing windows at either end. In the middle are French doors leading to a half-circle balcony, big enough for only one person to stand on. A large, tiled, private bathroom with storage closet opens off the end by the fireplace. I have converted the space into three living areas: bedroom/TV room at the window seat end; study/office at the fireplace end, and "tea room" with a drop-leaf table and chairs in front of the French doors, where I sit and grade papers from my part-time job as a community college English instructor, pausing from time to time to admire the trees just beyond my balcony. I share the downstairs kitchen, dining room and living room with Pam.

The third floor of this house contains another kitchen, bathroom and three bedrooms. Andy, a middle-aged antique book dealer, and Rob, a young clerk in the independent bookstore half a block away, live up there. Andy is a genuine "cat whisperer" who takes care of Daisy and Felix when I am away on trips to visit my children or explore faraway places. Mark, a former technical writer who is working on a novel, shares the second floor with me and handles the bookings of tenants. In addition to my rooms, the second floor contains two more bedrooms and another bath. Since I've been here, we've also had two short-term tenants from France: a young man from Paris attending a special program at Washington University, and a female Ph.D. computer analyst from Lyon, here on a four-month research grant. Pam sleeps in an apartment in the basement that she is still in the process of constructing for herself.

Once a month, I go to poetry readings at the Welsh pub half a block from my house; several times I've even read my own poetry there. Although I seldom eat in the Central West End restaurants (most are out of my price range), my old friend George, who lives about a block away, often walks with me three blocks down Euclid Ave. to get a frozen yogurt at Fro-Yo. I can walk almost everywhere I want to go now— library, church, post office doctor's office, grocery store, drugstore, bus stop, MetroLink, even the AA Club, which is right next door to the bishop's mansion where Pope John Paul II stayed when he visited St. Louis in January of 1999.

I haven't had that dream about houses since I moved here, but the thought sometimes occurs to me: Is it because I'm dreaming now? At this point in my life, I'm no longer sure.

Note: Shortly after this essay was finished, I found I wasn't as suited to communal living as I had hoped, so I moved again. The cats and I are now living in a very pleasant 2-bedroom apartment in a more working class neighborhood in South St. Louis. The 550-apartment complex is beautifully landscaped, with lots of tall trees, rosebushes and other plants, and there is a large and lovely park across the street. I sincerely hope we can stay here until I have to be carted off to the nursing home or St. Louis University Medical School, where I have prearranged to donate my body.

Thursday

Author's note: This, too, is fiction. We never had a family room, and I was never married to a TV anchor. In fact, in the newspaper world where my former husband and my brother worked, TV anchors were generally regarded with some distain, as pretty faces with largely empty heads.

It had been a bad winter so far. Outside, snow was falling lightly, and the temperature was near zero. In the family room, Laura lay wrapped in a blanket on the couch, half-asleep, lulled by the sound of her husband's voice as he anchored the nightly news and keeping awake only to listen for the TV weather report. Would it snow again tomorrow? It mustn't snow tomorrow! Tomorrow was Thursday, and Thursday comes, unfortunately, only once a week. Thursday. What an agony of waiting from one week to the next.

If she were lucky, class times could become so absorbing on other days of the week that, for an hour or two at a time, she could forget about Thursdays. But, too often, when her students were bent over their desks trying to put something on paper that would satisfy her for Composition 101, she wandered (to all appearances idly) to the window to gaze out at the parking lot. Did anyone notice that her eyes roamed restlessly down the rows until they lighted on the little brown second-hand Mercedes or, as was sometimes the case, she turned away quickly because it was not there?

During the rest of the week she cooked meals, took the children to their lessons, made love to her husband and graded her papers like any other housewife-mother-teacher, but she was waiting for Thursday. And sometimes Thursday came and went and brought her nothing more than an agonizing longing for another week to pass.

Wednesdays were the very worst. That was the day she found out what Thursday would bring. That was when she was obliged to wait, distracted and tense, all morning and into the last five minutes of her work day, for him to call. And because he often didn't call, she had to make the decision once more to call him—or not.

Once in awhile, pride or anger got the upper hand, and she walked to her car and drove home without calling. But, most of the time, she called. And just the sound of his voice—the gruff, slightly impatient hello, then the tantalizing West Indian lilt of his voice when he had recognized her own—made everything better. But her heart didn't stop pounding or her hands relax until the question had been asked and answered.

"What's the weather report?" she would ask in her best effort at nonchalance. And if he said, "Tomorrow is going to be a rainy day," she was glad that he couldn't see her face, so that she could keep up the pretense of casualness. But, more often, she could feel him smile as he replied, "The weather report is good. The sun is going to shine," and she knew that tomorrow, at least, would be all right.

If it didn't snow. Everyone knew how much she dreaded driving on ice and snow, and it was a long way to her college in another town. It it were too bad—and this winter's weather had been exceptionally bad— her family simply would not understand her choosing to drive so many miles on slick and dangerous roads just for office hours.

That was the story she told them: Thursdays were for office hours. She simply avoided telling them that the sign on the door said, "Thursday afternoon from 1 to 4 p.m." Thus she had a whole morning, once a week, to spend with him.

And golden hours they were, those mornings with just the two of them. There in his rooms she could escape all the pressures of her daily life: children's exhausting and frightening adolescence, husband's problems at work, worries about money and approaching middle age. For a few hours each week, she lived the life she had always dreamed about.

Music was always playing softly on the reel-to-reel tape player when she arrived, and it was exactly the kind she loved: Hubert Laws, George Benson, the Modern Jazz Quartet. It was almost laughably perfect. He must had read every book on the art of seduction. Or else he was a natural.

Only he hadn't seduced her. She was the one who had made the first move. They had spent a year having occasional lunches together with other faculty members, laughingly making suggestive remarks to one another, all in fun. Until one day she had asked him to have lunch with her in the little town alone. When she made another casual pass, he said, "I never know how to take what you say," and she had replied solemnly, "I'm serious."

When one is a housewife watching the years speed by, one can't wait forever for Fate to smile. Sometimes one has to twist the lady's arm. He could afford to be patient because he was younger and single and graced with most of the attributes women find attractive. But Laura couldn't wait.

For reasons that never ceased to delight her, he had responded with interest to her advances. And she was grateful—more than he could know. Those hours on Thursday morning couldn't possibly have the meaning for him that they held for her. There were other girls in his life; he didn't try to hide it. After all, she was a married woman with children and no intention of breaking up her home. He couldn't very well be expected to build his life around a few hours a week with an older, married woman.

Still, when he mentioned a girlfriend in passing or told her as she admired his shirt that it was a present from a girl, she felt a clutch in her chest that she could neither explain nor share.

So it was really an exaggeration to say that all the hours were golden. There were moments when the outside world intruded and threw a gloom over everything, which she was obliged to try to hide in a show of light-hearted interest in his life beyond their time together.

But when he lay half-comatose in her arms after lovemaking, when her arms were around him and she could feel his heartbeat and his deep, regular breathing brush her ear, she felt that she could lie there forever with his weight upon her rather than sacrifice one moment of such contentment. It was as if a rare and beautiful butterfly had landed on her hand.

And when she sat in his tiny kitchen watching him move around the room, bouncing lightly on the balls of his feet in time to the music as he brewed a pot of their favorite tea, happiness filled her like warm sunshine.

She loved to sit on the edge of the tub and watch him soap his glistening, muscular arms and legs. Washing his back for him, she tried to think of ways to slow time down. And when he stepped from the tub and dried himself carefully, she rubbed oil all over his lithe, brown body to keep his skin smooth and so nice for love, Being with him was like stepping through the looking glass into another world once a week. They had been born a country, a culture, a race, and a decade apart, and she was seized by a passion to know him.

Perhaps that was what appealed to him most, for although he was what some would call a "private person," when they were together he revealed a secret desire to be known. There was a reticence about him that made him withhold details of his daily life, and yet at times he would launch into an orgy of self-revelation. He showed her his college yearbooks and the medals he had won and newspaper clippings about the island of his birth. And he told her stories of his childhood, so different from her own.

The best part was that he was always changing: Their lovemaking never fell into a pattern. Sometimes, he was serious and reserved, and on other occasions, he was as carefree and playful as a small boy. "Let's get under the covers and tell stories," he had once said, after lighting a little kerosene lamp on the bedside table. At such times she loved him with almost all of her heart.

She realized that he didn't know much about her current life, even though she, too, shared stories of her childhood. Coming from a life of sun-drenched island poverty, he probably thought she was wealthy because her husband, an older man in whose shadow she had lived, was a well-known local newscaster. His experience hadn't yet taught him how slight the correlation between local celebrity and real money could be. He had never seen her home, and he never would. She valued her family too much to risk its dissolution by bringing a lover to the house.

He knew, of course, that she was crazy about her children. But how could she explain that she adored them to the point that, for years, she had endured the dull ache of a flawed marriage rather than shatter the picture of a happy little family and see her children shunted to their father on weekends?

And how could she possibly explain her deep feeling for her husband—an affection that had survived and even grown, despite the fact that their temperaments and expectations had been sadly mismatched?

She and her husband had known moments of joy. They had created and raised children together. And though they had realized early in their marriage that something was missing, such was their mutual desire for stability and continuity of family life that they had shared the knowledge with no one. To everyone they were a "perfect couple." And in a sense they thought so themselves. Her husband was a member of her family. She admired, loved, and respected him. How could she explain that to her lover?

So she must keep it light. Pretend not to be bothered when he forgot to call, or when "business" prevented him from keeping their appointment. Listen patiently and with understanding when he spoke of other women or shared with her his dream of getting a better job and leaving this town forever. Or, worse yet, returning to the land of his birth.

She had no hope of a future with him. She knew that. One must be grateful for small favors and grasp the golden moments whenever one can.

*   *   *

The room was dark except for the glow of the TV screen. The children were in their rooms upstairs, studying or watching TV, and the house was quiet and cold.

After her husband's familiar, handsome face disappeared from the screen, the weather forecaster appeared to announce an impending blizzard and to advise against unnecessary travel tomorrow. So, wrapping herself more tightly in the blanket, cocoon-like, and, turning her face to the back of the couch, Laura prepared to wait another week until Thursday.

Love Hostage

You are the mirror
in which I catch
my fleeting image,
audience for my best plays,
auditor of all my accounts,
oral historian,
my magician,
repeatedly producing me
out of your hat,
bloodlessly sawing me in half,
then miraculously
making me whole again.

Tiger Eyes

One half-crazy aunt noticed
with exaggerated surprise
that in the headlights' beams
Laura's glow-in-the dark eyes
were amazingly like a cat's
when she was a little girl
of only two or three.

While dining years later
with her lover beside her
she discovered that her birth
was in the Year of the Tiger,
a time—alas!—when her fate had been sealed
although all that had yet to be revealed.

What Laura didn't know about cats back then
was that the overworked and neglected female
was the hunter who had to provide the prey
for the hungry cubs and the prowling he-male.
But it didn't take long for her to learn
enough to make her passions burn.

As the cubs grew older and her load grew lighter
the fire in her eyes grew noticeably brighter
and she started to scan the distant horizon
For something she had been longing to lay her eyes on.

She was searching for somebody strong and bold
to be her long-sought, coveted equal—
someone who would turn out to be, she hoped,
an absorbing challenge and amusing sequel
to the days of service and silent waiting
when her back was sore and her heart was aching.

She'd know him when she saw him, she thought,
but it shouldn't come as a great surprise
that she didn't recognize him at all
when first he appeared to her restless eyes,
for he was a tiger, too, you see,
and wily in the ways that tigers must be.

Like A Cat

LIke a cat dragging its prey to the master's doorstep,
I brought my proudest accomplishments home to you.
Like a child with a good report card,
I held up my high marks for your review.

A Scheherazade spinning nightly tales with death-defying art,
I plotted the play of my hungry life
and gave you the leading part.

All that mattered was your love.

Like a potentate lolling in Orient splendor
You accepted my trophies as your just due.
Like the parent of a precocious child,
you saw in my high marks a reflection of you.

A spider patiently waiting in a steely, invisible snare,
You took everything in and made it your own
and left me with empty arms there.

All you lost, then, was my love.

Coats

My daughter Tamara, who has done a fair amount of research on the subject of memory, tells me that it's very unreliable, so I'm going way out on a limb here to say that the first coat I remember owning was sewn by my Great Aunt Nell. Aunt Nell was actually my mother's aunt, and she went blind from glaucoma at around age 40—several years before I was born. All of us in Mom's family are extremely near-sighted, and Mom told me she used to practice the piano with her eyes closed, so that when she went blind like her Aunt Nell, she would still be able to play. Mom never went blind, but she was comforted by the thought that, if she ever did, she should be able to cope as well as her aunt. Among other things, Aunt Nell could sew on her machine, using spools of thread that Uncle Doran had notched for her to indicate the colors. To be perfectly honest, I can't see in my mind's eye the coat that she sewed for me when I was maybe four years old, but I remember telling myself, all my life, that it was made of some kind of pile, like fake fur. What I do remember, very vividly, is Aunt Nell at my grandmother's graveside, just before they lowered the casket, running her hands over Grandma's face so that she could have one last look at her baby sister.

The first coat I can clearly remember was a brown tweed cape, sewn for me by a lady in our church who was an especially good seamstress. One of the traditions in our very tightly knit church community was that all the little girls got new outfits, head to toe, on Easter Sunday. While my mother usually made mine, the Easter of the brown cape happened when my brother John was small and Mom was going to school and co-pastoring the church, so she was probably just too tired to sew for me. That year, Sister Hester (we called all of our members "Brother" or "Sister") made me an outfit consisting of a satin blouse with full sleeves, a skirt, a vest, and a cape. I still have a photo of me in that cape, wearing a brown beret over my tight little Shirley Temple brown curls and looking very pleased with myself. (As it turned out, the blouse was the part I liked best. I wore it so much that, one day, it disappeared. Some time later, I discovered that Mom had been leaving it in the bottom of the laundry basket because she was tired of seeing me wear it.)

Mom had a special fondness for capes. She had several of her own over the years, and she made capes for other members of the family. When Harold and I moved our family to Ohio in 1969, she made

capes for our girls to wear that Easter. I cherish a photo of the three of them in their wide-brimmed hats, capes, and patent-leather shoes, gripping their Easter baskets and frowning into the sun. After her retirement from teaching junior high music and math in East St. Louis, Illinois, Mom went to Paraguay to teach in an interdenominational school there, and she brought back a brown-and-white alpaca cape for me. I no longer have that cape, but I still have a jewel-green, floor-length velvet one that Mom sewed for me perhaps 30 years ago. When I was still working, I used to wear it on infrequent formal occasions, usually around the Christmas holidays. Recently, when I directed a reading of a play for my readers theatre group, the actor who played the superhero wore that cape, along with my elbow-length black gloves, and we all got a big laugh out of it. But when I used to wear the cape on formal occasions, I felt conspicuously elegant and enveloped in Mom's love. She wasn't a demonstrative mother—in fact, she could be very harsh—but she showed her love for people by doing things for them. She tried to tell me that when I was growing up, but I never fully appreciated it until she was almost gone. Now, I look back at all the dresses she sewed for me, as well as other things like the ruffled taffeta bedspread that she designed herself—not to mention the quilts she hand-stitched for every member of her family, including her seven siblings, her two children, and her grandchildren—and I see the unspoken love that went into all of them.

When I turned 15, I went through a very traumatic experience involving an aborted elopement to Arkansas with a boy from our church who was six years my senior. Fed by gossip, that incident ballooned into a major partisan dispute among our church members, with accusations flying in all directions, and it eventually led to the breakup of our congregation. In the midst of all the turmoil, my Grandma Rainbolt bought me a rather stylish blue-gray, wraparound coat of the nubbly texture that was popular in the 1950s. I still have a photo of myself in that coat and the gray sweater and yellow-and-gray pleated skirt that my mother bought me to go with it. I think my Mom and Grandma were trying to tell me that, despite the trouble I had caused, I was still a protected member of the family.

The next summer, before my junior year of high school, Mom encouraged me to lie about my age so that I could get a job as a bill collator in the credit office at Famous-Barr department store in St. Louis where her sister Edith worked. Getting up early in the morning, I rode the bus from Belleville, Illinois, across the Mississippi to work eight hours a day, five days a week, for 75 cents an hour. While the extra income was more than welcome, since our church (and the "free will offerings" from members on which we relied) had been split in half over the scandal involving the aforementioned boy, I think Mom was mainly hoping the job would keep me too busy and tired to think about him. She said she used to go to Famous-Barr and ride the escalator to the 9th floor just so she could look down over the dividers on the 8th floor to see me working, and she felt sorry for me because I looked so tired. What she didn't know was that I was staying up half the night talking to that same boy through my bedroom window in a poor man's modern-day re-enactment of Shakespeare's classic love story that eventually ended less tragically than Romeo and Juliet, but tragically enough.

In the meantime, though, I used my 20 percent discount at Famous-Barr to buy myself a sporty, navy blue, double-breasted wool coat that was all the fashion back then and which made me feel more like my better-off classmates in the neighborhood when I wore it to school. I also bought a tailored jacket of soft, tan leather when such things were all the fashion, in which I felt especially cool.

By the time I went away to college at Oklahoma State University, I had almost put my first love behind me and was on my way to becoming engaged to a rather more suitable boy. As cold weather came on, I received a most unexpected package in the mail from my mother. In it was not only a black wool wraparound coat, which I didn't remember asking for, but also an ankle-length formal dress, which I definitely had not requested and never would have expected in a million years to receive from my mother. Our church strictly forbade dancing, and Mom had almost always tried to adhere to her frequent admonition to me: "Don't get yourself talked about." I say "almost always," because Mom had once defied the church's proscription against movies by taking me to a showing of "Gone With the Wind" when we were out of town visiting her baby sister. Also, when she periodically got totally fed up with her marriage or other frustrating situations, she was capable of creating scenes that the family is still talking about, so she had a hard time following her own advice. Anyway, I, who had always found the "don't get yourself talked about" advice strangely perverse if not downright hypocritical, would always reply, "If people talk about me, that's a reflection on them, not me!" So perhaps you can imagine my utter confusion at my mother's gift of a formal gown, which could only be interpreted as permission to attend school dances, something I had never done in high school, where I had been obliged to sit in the bleachers while my classmates learned to dance in gym class. There was no explanatory note in the package. Still somewhat dazed by Mom's totally uncharacteristic behavior, I wore that gown to the first—and only—school dance that I ever attended—with the boy to whom I later became engaged but never married. The coat that had accompanied the formal came in very handy when those cutting Oklahoma winds came sweeping down the plains that year, bringing a near-blizzard in April of 1957.

While still in high school, I had occasionally played dress-up with the leopard-skin coat Mom's youngest sister, Aunt Bess, had brought back from her stint as a missionary India. I assume that was before leopards became a protected species and I know it was long before my consciousness had been raised enough to appreciate the leopard's sacrifice. While I still love the feel of fur, I now prefer to enjoy it while it's still attached to the animal. Besides, that leopard coat was extremely heavy, and the fur didn't feel at all silky—perhaps because the skins had been poorly prepared. But wearing leopard back then probably made my mom, who had been poor all her life, feel exotically elegant.

As for elegance, I was always attracted to it, even when the fur was fake. During the first years of my marriage, we had so little money that most of my coats from that period have long since faded from memory, except for one: At a department store sale in St. Louis, I found a coat buried among a bunch of other items where it didn't seem to belong, as if it had been hidden away there, just for me. It was a deep scarlet wool with a flared skirt, black fake-fur collar and cuffs, and huge crocheted black buttons that made me feel like a Russian princess, straight out of "War and Peace." I fell in love with that coat in the same way I had fallen for my first pair of red high-heeled shoes. Do you suppose that means I'm really a scarlet woman at heart? I had to buy it, of course, and wore it for years.

Several years later, not too long before my husband and I separated and while we were on a rare shopping trip together, he impulsively bought me a calf-length flared coat that was reversible: khaki poplin on one side and fake heather-colored fur on the other. Not only did that coat serve as excellent protection from bitterly windy days, but, with the fur turned inside, it was also a great coverall for naps on the couch by the fireside. I still savor the memory of tucking my feet in the fur-lined hood to keep them toasty warm.

Coats were pretty much an afterthought during the period when I lived in the year-round sunshine of Phoenix after my second divorce, but upon my return to St. Louis in 1989 to be near my aging and ill parents, I realized that I was going to need something to protect me against the Midwest winters. I found just what I was looking for on sale at a Dillard's department store: A gun-metal nylon number, the crumpled texture of which looked like leather at first glance. It was rain-and wind-resistant and weighed next to nothing, but it had a zip-out lining that made it surprisingly warm. On a trip to New York City in the 1990s, it kept me warm in below-zero temperatures as I toured Wall Street and other attractions of the Big Apple, trailed by a crazy Chinese woman who had attached herself to me at the youth hostel near Columbia University where I was staying for $10 a night. I was unnaturally attached to that coat, as much for its utility as for its looks, and I wore it steadily for the next 20 years, using it as a coverall for naps and rolling it into a ball for a pillow on long international and cross-country flights. It was my Linus blanket, which became kind of a joke to my family and friends. It eventually became so shabby that I reluctantly had to replace it. The black, double-breasted, all-weather coat that I bought at Saks to replace it cost a lot more, but it just isn't the same. I thought the removable black fur trim on the hood of the new coat was elegant, but I knew my daughters Julia and Titi would give me no end of grief for wearing it, so it has remained in my drawer most of the time. Besides, the coat was made in China. I read somewhere that the Chinese sometimes use cat fur on the clothes they export, and, while I have never fact-checked that statement, the thought that a cat may have given its life for my vanity is enough to make me have second thoughts about having bought that coat, and I'm sure that if my daughters ever thought I was wearing cat fur, at least two of them would disown me for life.

More recently, though, I found a coat that may join the red coat with black fur trim, the reversible khaki with fur-lined hood, and the nylon all-purpose coat in my personal Coat Hall of Fame. It's a hip-length fake mouton, in perfect condition, that I found in a thrift store in Stillwater, Oklahoma, for the bargain price of just $20. Just before I moved to Oklahoma, my mom had died a very peaceful death in hospice care, so I decided to work as a volunteer for Karman Korner, a thrift shop in Stillwater that benefits a local hospice program. I found the mouton at the store on a visit to Oklahoma after my move back to St. Louis. At first I thought it was genuine and was ecstatic to learn, via Google, that second-hand moutons in good condition are worth between $75 and $250. A few weeks later, however, a friend discovered a tiny label in the coat saying that it was pure acrylic. No matter. It's a lovely, warm coat, and it reminds me of the wonderful hospice care Mom received. Unfortunately, thanks to global warming, I have had very few occasions to wear it during the past couple of winters.

After Mom's death, my Aunt Carolyn, of the leopard coat, became a kind of surrogate mother to me. She was 10 years younger than Mom, and they had a lot in common, although the relationship between them had been very similar to my own relationship with Mom: a tremendously powerful mixture of resentment, anger, admiration and love. Still, they had sung beautiful duets together, and Aunt Carolyn, who was an awesomely talented musician, never forgot that Mom had taught her to play the piano. If anyone could be more adventurous than Mom, it was Aunt Carolyn. In her late teens, she had gone off to the Kentucky Mountains as a missionary to the hill people, and a few years later, when I was around nine, she married an American missionary in India—much to my regret, as I had always aspired to be her flower girl. Two children, two more marriages and many international adventures later, she was the proud owner of a mink jacket, a present from her third and last husband. For about three years after Mom's death, she and I frequently exchanged emails, in which she would sometimes say how much she missed her big sister and at other times would tell me stories that cast Mom in unflattering light, making me think that sibling rivalry can continue well after the death of one of the siblings. Aunt Carolyn often mentioned that she wanted to leave her mink jacket to me in her will. By this time, I was a sporadic contributor to the World Wildlife Fund and not especially eager to be seen wearing dead animal pelts, but I didn't want to seem ungrateful, so I gently suggested that Aunt Carolyn's daughter-in-law or granddaughter might like to have it. She didn't take the hint, though, and few weeks after her death, I received a box containing the jacket—uninsured and carelessly packed, as if whoever had sent it—probably one of her husband's children—was grudgingly carrying out her last wishes. There was no note.

This gift presented me with a dilemma: Despite a nagging feeling that excessive wealth is unfair and possibly even sinful, I do have an attraction to nice things, and although I dearly love animals, I also enjoy the luxurious feeling of being swathed in fur. So I conducted an informal poll, via Facebook, of friends and family: Should I wear it, give it away, or what? Responses were mixed. Several people pointed out that, since the animals in question were long dead, I couldn't be accused of causing their untimely demise. "Wear it!" they said. On the other side, my youngest daughter, a self-described "crazy cat lady," was emphatically against my wearing it. My middle daughter, the philosopher, informed me that minks raised for fur suffer a particularly grisly fate, being electrocuted by a rod thrust up their anus to avoid damaging their fur, and that wearing the coat would be tacitly condoning that practice. I never checked to see if this information was accurate, but I was sufficiently appalled to lose a good deal of enthusiasm for the whole mink coat thing. When I informed my eldest that the two other girls had said I shouldn't wear it, her laconic response was, "Well, I guess I know who will inherit it from you." A dog-owner and animal lover, she nevertheless fell into the camp maintaining that the pelts of long-dead animals might as well be put to good use.

So I brokered a deal with my eldest. A few years earlier, I had talked her into buying a black cashmere coat with wildly fluffy angora collar and cuffs which she had scarcely, if ever, worn. Although she acknowledged that it was beautiful, and I thought she looked gorgeous in it, her taste—like that of my other two daughters—is significantly less flamboyant than my own, and she felt overdressed in it. So I offered to trade her the mink for the cashmere, and she agreed. My guess is that she has never worn the mink and only consented to trade because she wanted to do something nice for me, which makes me love her—and my black cashmere coat—all the more.

In my declining years, with several coats in my closet now, I sincerely doubt that I will ever need to purchase or receive another, but I have enough good coat memories to last me the rest of my life.

Flashback

Some secret wisdom kept me from making
home movies of my babies.
Nostalgia's poor protection against panic.
Paging idly through old photographs one day,
I saw their three small forms spread out on a blanket in the sun—
little perfect faces laughing toward the camera,
round, soft baby bodies,
hair as fine as spider silk—

I could hardly stand to look.

Never mind that in their places are three young beauties—
lively, strong, living out my dreams in all directions.
This, too, is joy, and it will pass, and someday will be only
pictures in a book.

Motherhood

My mom wasn't crazy about motherhood, I suspect. As the eldest of eight children, she had more than her share of child care responsibilities growing up, and from the stories she told, it didn't sound like fun. Moreover, she was already well launched in a career as a lady preacher when she met my dad. Still, she always maintained that she had prayed for four years to get pregnant with me. She was putting a little spin on the truth, apparently, since I was born less than four years after she married my dad. My guess is that she was worried about what the church people would think if she didn't have a baby—would they think she was using birth control? Or maybe she was afraid she would lose Dad if she didn't have children with him, although that doesn't seem likely, since she told me more than once that they had been very happy before I was born. Maybe the truth was imbedded in the little story she often told me: "When you were born, I said to myself, 'Now I have someone to love me just for myself.'" When she would say that, I would always respond, "But, Mom, that's the way a mother loves a child—not the other way around."

Mom sometimes complained that when I was a baby, Dad would go off with his friends, leaving her alone to care for me—and me for her—but as far back as I can remember—and even farther, from what I was told—I received a lot of care from people in my parents' church. Whether that was because they felt sorry for me or I was just an utterly charming baby and toddler, I can't say, but I would like to think the latter is true. One woman in our church was like a second mother to me and undoubtedly a major reason that I made it through childhood without more psychological scars. I always knew her by "Ray," which was actually her last name. I heard her real first name once but quickly forgot it. What I never forgot was that she gave me unconditional love.

Ray had two teenage daughters of her own when she started caring for me, and Mom thought she spoiled them because she would do the dishes for them so they wouldn't ruin their manicures. Although we moved away from the little Texas town where Ray lived when I was two-and-a-half years old, I went back there several times on vacation when I was growing up. The first time was probably the summer after my little brother, John, was born, when I was nine years old. While I was visiting her, I got a rare opportunity to go swimming. A lot of our church members back then didn't approve of mixed bathing, but Ray was more laid back and not averse to breaking a rule that didn't make sense to her. Using a playsuit pattern, she sewed me a terrycloth swimsuit and walked with me every day to the city swimming pool. On our way, we would pass the home of Sister Cornelius, a pillar of the church who was famous for having been the Sunday School teacher of several boys who grew up to be preachers. "Hello, Sister Cornelius," Ray would call sweetly to the old lady sitting on the front porch as we passed, "We're just going out for a little walk." After we reached the pool, having gone a roundabout way so Sister Cornelius wouldn't suspect anything, Ray would sit outside the fence and watch me paddle around in the shallow end until I was ready to leave. When she put me on the train to go back home that first year, there were tears in my eyes.

The next summer when I went for a visit, while Mom was still suffering from what we would now call postpartum depression, Texas was having a drought and the pool was closed. Ray's house wasn't air-conditioned—only the rich had air conditioning back then—but she made sure I was comfortable on her bed in front of the window fan, which threw out tiny droplets of water. I spent whole afternoons there reading comic books from a big pile she had thoughtfully set beside the bed. When I was at their house, Mama Ray and Papa Ray made sure I had everything I liked to eat: cornbread, longhorn cheese, watermelon, enchiladas, and salmon croquettes, dipped in cornmeal and fried.

I had only three or four vacations at Ray's, but they were lifesavers. I guess you could say she was a natural-born mother. In her old age, when she decided it was time to go to the nursing home, she made all the arrangements and moved in without telling her daughters until everything was settled because she didn't want them to try to talk her out of it. One summer when my daughters were teenagers, I had a powerful and persistent urge to go to Texas to visit her in that home, but I was taking my middle daughter to ice-skating lessons several times a week and told myself the trip would have to wait until the summer session was over. Before it ended, I received word from one of Ray's daughters that she had died. But the memory of her unselfish love has sustained me through more than one rough spot in life.

As a mother, I probably fell somewhere between my own mother and Ray in terms of selfless devotion. I didn't grow up pining to be a mother or have babies, and I wasn't especially crazy about baby dolls, although I was very disappointed one Christmas when I failed to receive the drink 'n wet doll I had requested from Santa Claus (even though I already knew he wasn't real) and I was thrilled on another Christmas Eve when I sneaked downstairs in the middle of the night to discover a beautiful blonde bride doll standing beneath the tree. In general, though, I didn't play much with dolls, and I didn't think babies were nearly as cute as people kept saying they were—some of them were downright unattractive, in my view. But I did fall in love with two of them when I was still a child: first, my cousin, "Little Jim," who lived next door, and then my brother.

Little Jim was born three years after me, and while he was still a toddler, my mother used to send me over to her brother Jim's house in the early mornings while she went to sing and play on a religious radio program. Uncle Jim, who was a carpenter, would already be gone to work, but Aunt Elsie, who was barely out of her teens, would still be in bed with Little Jim, and I would crawl in with them. The two of us would have fun playing with Little Jim and dressing him in doll clothes. When he was still pretty small, he often amused us by doing funny things like taking a map to his mother and asking her to show him where hell was. I adored him and I was really upset when, by the age of six or so, he decided he was too big to be hugged and wouldn't let me cuddle him anymore.

My only sibling, John, was born on July 23, 1947, a very hot month in a very hot summer, when I was almost nine years old. New mothers had to stay in the hospital for a week back then, and children weren't allowed as visitors, so I could only stand on the roof of our car to wave at Mom as she looked out the hospital window, and I didn't get to see my brother until she brought him home. My first memory of him is leaning over his crib, which was covered with mosquito netting, to breathe in the sweet smell of baby lotion and talcum powder. As my mother often said later, I took over as John's mother almost immediately. I changed his diapers and walked him when he had the colic.

Once, when he was a toddler, my mom and I were doing dishes and I started to worry because I hadn't seen him for awhile. I asked if I  could go look for him, but she thought I was trying to get out of drying the dishes. Finally, when the tears started rolling down my cheeks, she said, "Oh, I'll go!" and headed upstairs to look for him. A moment later, I heard her say "Oh, Pat!" He had eaten a whole bottle of Carter's Little Liver Pills. There was no poison control center in those days, and the doctor's office was closed. When we finally reached him by phone, he said we should try to make him vomit, and if he developed any symptoms, we should take him to the emergency room. I stuck my finger down his throat, he threw up, and he didn't develop any problems. Another time, when he was still a preschooler, he sneaked out of the house one morning, got in the neighbor's jeep and released the brake, causing it to roll downhill and hit a tree. My parents weren't home, so I rode in the neighbor's car with him to the doctor, who put stitches in his head. I rode him in the basket of my bicycle and took him for rides in our car long before I was old enough to drive legally (my dad had taught me to drive when I was nine), and when I started dating, I even took him on some of my dates. If a boy didn't like my little brother, that was a strike against him in my eyes. And, unlike my cousin Jimmy, my little brother never stopped letting me hug and kiss him.

Despite my maternal feelings toward these two little boys, though, I didn't spend any time dreaming about getting married and becoming a mother. I was more interested in having a career—first as a dress designer, until I discovered that I didn't like sewing; then, briefly, as a lady preacher, before my interest in religion started to become ambivalent; then as a classical flutist; an actor; a famous writer; and, by the time I entered college, an architect, although being a blues singer was always a longing locked away in my heart.

I did have a rather prophetic daydream when I was around 11 or 12, though. I saw myself as the mother of four beautiful and talented daughters. I even picked out names for three of them: Cynthia, Sylvia, and Deborah. I imagined that when they were grown, people would look at me and say, "There's Pat, the mother of those four beautiful daughters!" It seemed almost like magic to me years later when I actually had three beautiful, brilliant and talented daughters, and while they aren't named Cynthia, Sylvia, and Deborah, two of them do have names that end in "a." There have been a lot of strange things in my life like that. Sometimes I'm almost afraid to daydream, for fear that I might actually be planning my own fate.

Although motherhood was not at the top of my list of ambitions as I was growing up, that changed somewhat when I started getting involved with boys. I still had career ambitions, but I don't know whether it was because I had read too many novels or listened to too many co-dependent love songs (of which there was a glut in the 1940s and '50s by some of my favorite singers, like Nat King Cole), but from the time I became sexually active (which was way too early), I always had a strong desire to "make a baby" with the object of my passion. As far as I can tell, it was more of an urge to merge than a desire to take on the responsibilities of motherhood. I had always assumed that this was a common biological instinct, but my eldest daughter tells me she never had such feelings, so maybe I was more like my mother than I realized; maybe I just wanted someone to love me for myself.

At 18, I met a man seven years my senior who captured my imagination, so I proposed and he accepted, and nine months and three weeks after the wedding, our first little girl was born. Tamara was a source of perpetual wonder to me—and anxiety. Once when she was only a few weeks old, I tried to clip her paper-thin fingernails and accidentally nipped her skin, causing it to bleed. I cried more than she did, and for days I anxiously watched her arm for telltale signs of blood poisoning. But while I loved her more than I had ever dreamed I was capable of doing, I was determined not to have any more children after having experienced the physical shock of giving birth.

Marilyn ("Titi") was born 17 months later, and Julia followed 25 months after that. So, in a little over four years, I went from being a carefree, single college student to a mother of three. It didn't help that I was married to a man who was born old. He was helpful with the children during the day when he was home but hopeless once he had gone to sleep at night. And he had no interest in some of the things I still longed to do, like skate, swim, ride bikes, listen to jazz and take long rides in the country.

As anyone who has raised a baby knows, they are a lot of work, and the word "work" had always been anathema to me. The daughter of a harsh but hard-working German father, my mother often seemed to value work above everything else, and she could be exasperatingly irrational about it, which is probably the main reason I was allergic to the word. Once when I was growing up, she attacked me for not doing

the dishes. "But I did the dishes!" I protested. "The dishes aren't done until the floor has been swept," she declared with finality. Another time, she called my elementary school and had me walk a mile home on my lunch hour to make my bed because I had failed to make it before I left. "One good thing about Dad was that he taught us how to work," she and her siblings were fond of saying. So it was a genuine revelation to me when, having crawled out of bed one time around 2 a.m. to feed the newest baby, I realized that I loved the three of them so passionately precisely because I was responsible for them, despite all the hard work involved.

Always keenly aware of the ironic twists in life, I became hyper-vigilant as a mother, perpetually on the lookout for disaster. How could I be so lucky? What if the house caught on fire? What if one of the girls got the croup? What if there was a gas leak? Before becoming a mother, I could sleep through a tornado or a train wreck. Afterwards, things were never the same. I couldn't sleep, I couldn't relax, and, to my husband's intense disappointment, I lost most of my interest in sex—except when I was pregnant.

Once I came to terms with the fact that I was pregnant again, I would turn into a sex machine for a few months, feeling like Mother Earth as my belly and breasts distended. I was thrilled to feel the baby moving inside me and loved trying to identify its elbows or heels from the irregular bumps on my tummy. It helped significantly that my husband was not one of those men who are turned off by pregnant women. He thought the whole process was as sexy as I did and called me his "Reuben's nude." Sometimes, after a particularly good session of lovemaking, I would go into the children's bedroom to kiss my sleeping babies, thinking about how they were the miraculous products of this passion.

During my first pregnancy, I worried a lot about whether I would be able to love a new baby as much as I had loved my little brother, but by the time the third was born, I realized that my heart was an elastic organ, with plenty of room to love as many children as I might have, although I still desperately wanted to stop having them. Coming home from the hospital after the birth of my second baby, I burst into tears when I saw my 17-month-old staring at me with wide eyes as if to say, "I thought you had gone away forever." In the five days I had been gone, she seemed to have gone from a baby to a little girl.

Watching my babies grow and learn was, for me, like watching the development of the human race. Although they remember me fussing at them about the messes they made, I marveled at their stunning creativity in making amazingly realistic costumes out of scarves, bedsheets and whatever came to hand, and erecting buildings out of tables and overturned chairs. When they were a little older, I took them to the Goodwill to buy formals to play dress-up, and by the time they were in school, they started playing "boarding school," a game that could go on for hours, or even days. During these games, their dad and I were the "staff," cautioned to keep in character, even at mealtimes, and speak only when spoken to.

Always fond of exploration myself, I took the girls on long drives in the country to charming little tea shops for lunch and area parks for picnics. I pulled them out of school at noon to dine with me at the Big Boy or the local bowling alley—sometimes all together, sometimes one at a time. I wrote excuses to their teachers so we could attend a coffee concert featuring the Dayton Ballet Company and the Dayton Philharmonic, and once, when I thought our furnace was giving off suspicious fumes, I hauled them out of bed in the middle of the night to take them to the local drive-in restaurant while Harold stayed home to greet the gas man, who had been called to check for leaks. They got to sleep in the next morning, even though it was a school day.

There were lessons of all kinds—swimming, gymnastics, art, tap dancing, ballet, piano, violin, guitar, acting, creative writing—and summer camp for the two younger ones. (Tamara, a dedicated ballet dancer, never took to roughing it in the great outdoors.) And when they graduated from high school, I took each daughter to Europe—just the two of us—going to as many countries as we could afford on our limited budget, staying in B&Bs and traveling on Eurail passes.

In between times, all of us, including Harold, took family vacations—a couple of times on the retirement money I had collected after quitting one of my many jobs. We drove to the West Coast, DC, Hilton Head, and Canada, among other places, and once the girls and I took a road trip to Texas with my mother, stopping to see my mom's old friends from her days in Waxahachie and the daughter of my beloved Ray in Electra.

I loved those three girls more than anything in life. But sometimes, when the days of washing diapers and getting up in the middle of the night seemed to extend forward into eternity, I lay in bed and longed to be out in the fields where I had spent some of the most carefree times of my childhood, listening to the cows munch on the grass while a plane hummed overhead. At such times, I felt like a prisoner.

At other times, my nerves would snap and I would treat my babies harshly. Once, when Tamara resisted bedtime by repeatedly calling for a drink of water, I went in and poured part of a glass of water on her head. It probably wasn't more than a couple of tablespoons, but she was shocked, and I shouldn't have done it. Around the time Julia, our third baby, was born, Titi, our second, who had been a most docile and sweet baby, began to be very cranky and difficult during the day. At night she would climb out of her crib over and over to come to me when I was trying to nurse Julia or get some much-needed rest. Feeling exhausted and exasperated, I would hit her on the bottom, hard. We later learned that she was suffering from a congenital urethra problem that caused her to have repeated bladder infections, for which she had two hospitalizations and was on medication for six years. The memory of my harsh response to that poor baby who was undoubtedly in pain and looking for comfort from her mother is the worst shame of my life—something for which I will never be able to forgive myself. Remembering it, I always think of a line from James Baldwin in *Notes of a Native Son*: "When one slapped one's child in anger the recoil in the heart reverberated through heaven and became part of the pain of the universe."

Although I think that was my greatest sin as a mother, I have had second thoughts, too, about my decision to place my daughters in inner-city schools where the student population was more than 90 percent African American in the turbulent years of the early 1970s, when racial tensions were so high. "I would never do that to my children," my mother told me more than once. But, having grown up with a strong sense of the injustices that African Americans had suffered throughout our nation's history, I was overwhelmed by a need to try to make a difference. I saw photos in the newspapers of little black children in Mississippi and Alabama walking through gauntlets of jeering whites to integrate southern schools, and I felt I could do no less than those brave black mothers who had risked their children's lives to try to change the world for the better. It wasn't easy on my girls, and I'm not sure they have ever totally forgiven me for it, but they understand racism at a gut level, having experienced it personally, and I am more than proud to say that they all have a strong sense of social justice for people of all races.

I did what I could to soften the experience for them, picking them up after school when they were in danger of being taunted by the meaner kids on the way home, and questioning them frequently about what was going on in school. It would be fair to say that I was a fanatic, though, and my children were the ones who had to pay the price. I wasn't aware until years later how big a price it was. I was pained to hear one of them confess, as an adult, that, sometimes during those years, she had fervently wished she was black. If I had it to do over again, knowing what I know now, I'm not sure I would have the nerve to do it again. I can only say that my intentions were good.

To be fair, their experience wasn't all negative. They had a few very good teachers, and while they tended to gravitate toward the one or two white students in their class, they did make some black friends, as well. Our middle daughter, "Titi," (short for "Tiger), who is smaller than her sisters by several inches—found the key to dealing with threats from the more hostile students. "You wait until the last day of school—I'm going to beat you up!" a student said to her one time. "Why wait until the last day?" she retorted. "Why not do it today?" No beating was forthcoming, and soon Titi made lots of friends of both races. When Harold and I separated while the two younger girls were still in high school, Titi was the one who elected to remain with her father in our integrated neighborhood and continue her education at the predominantly black high school, where she was on the gymnastics team. Our whole family often attended the girls' basketball games to cheer on the team and their fiercely successful African-American coach, Doris Black, whom Harold admiringly dubbed "Shut-the-gates-of-mercy Black" for her tendency to pour on the heat, even when the team was well ahead.

Although I have never stopped loving Harold, there were times, from the beginning of our marriage, when I was miserably unhappy with him, and I'm sure there were occasions when he felt the same. Maybe the differences in our ages and personalities were just too great; maybe we married before we got to know each other well enough; maybe we had children too soon and too close together. Maybe I was too young. Maybe we didn't have enough money. Whatever the reasons, our marriage began to fall apart when Julia, our youngest daughter, was 15, and by the time she graduated from high school, she and I were living together in an apartment in Kettering, Ohio, and I was beginning a career as a writer/editor.

When Harold and I separated, I suggested that, since he had always made twice as much money as I, he could send two daughters to college and I would send one, and that's what we did. But when Julia married in her junior year, I stopped supporting her financially. All my life, my mother had pounded into my head that when children are grown, they should be financially independent. Years later, it dawned on me that I had actually been less financially independent than my daughters at their age. Marrying at 19, I had a husband to support me (although I did work and/or go to school at least part-time for all but two of the years they were growing up), and after we were married, my parents had encouraged us to live in an apartment in their basement for a year so we could save our money for a downpayment on a home of our own, which we did. I regret now that I didn't give my daughters more financial support. I never made a high salary or accumulated any wealth, but I could have done more. I'm still shocked at how blind I was to the help I had received when I was young.

It was misguided good intentions, though, rather than lack of love, that caused me to be so hard on my children financially. A couple of years after my divorce from Harold, I was married briefly to another man, whose father informed me that one reason our marriage didn't last long was the fact that I loved my children too much. Although I have loved many people passionately over my 70-plus years—parents, children, my brother, and several men—I have concluded that learning *how* to love is one of the greatest challenges of life, and I am still working on mastering it.

While my children were growing up, I often heard the term "empty nest symptom," and I told myself I would never experience that problem, since the world is such a fascinating place to me that I would always find interesting things to do. But I'll never forget the sinking feeling I had the first time I stepped off a plane in Dayton, Ohio, upon returning home from a business trip and realized that there was no one left in town to be glad that I was home. By that time, Harold was working in Chicago, Julia was enrolled at Oklahoma State University, Titi was attending Earlham College in Indiana, and Tamara was attending Inter-American University in Puerto Rico. That was more than 30 years ago. We have never all lived in the same city again, and I still suffer pangs of empty nest syndrome, after all these years.

As my daughters were growing up, I had three wishes for them: I wanted them to be kind and ethical; I hoped they would be happy, and I thought it would be nice if they were successful at whatever they chose to do. I'm very proud to say that they are all good women, committed to noble causes. As I write this, Tamara R. Piety is a law professor and published author, Titi (M.G. Piety) is a philosophy professor and published author, and Julia Rieman is a partner in a law firm for which she writes—and her firm wins—an impressive number of appeals. I don't get to see them as often as I would like, but they have been good to me in many ways. For my 70th birthday, they took me on a road trip to Santa Fe, one of the highlights of my life as a mother.

I don't know how much difference my parenting made in how they turned out—they have all reminded me at one time or another that parents are not the only influence in a child's development—but I'm extremely pleased that they are all good and successful human beings, committed to humane causes. Whether they are happy is something only they can say, since happiness is hard to define and its intensity tends to fluctuate.

Men—and Women

I had girlfriends when I was growing up, and we had some good times, but I never had the kind of "best friend" that I so often hear women talk about. Looking back, I have to admit that I thought males were smarter and more interesting than most females, which is probably one reason I was the only girl in my mechanical drawing class in high school and one of approximately six girls among a thousand guys in my freshman engineering class at Oklahoma State University in 1952. I was in my 50s before I began to suspect that I had absorbed a bias in favor of men from my mother.

Mom had five brothers and two sisters. Her relationships with her sisters were close but rocky, while her relationships with her brothers were close. Period. For years, her brother Bill would call her every evening at 9 o'clock, and they would spend 30 minutes to an hour gossiping. I thought Uncle Bill, with his racist talk and dislike for Dad (he told Mom that Dad didn't love her), was a bad influence on Mom, and Dad apparently thought so, too. He told me once that when he could get Mom away from her family, she was a different person, more relaxed and easier to get along with.

But there was no getting Mom away from her family, especially her brothers. She and two of her brothers built our very first home. In later years, she invested money in some of the houses they built and shared in their profits. They never failed to come to her aid whenever she called them, and in her last years, when she was still living alone, at least one of them would come by her place to check on her almost every day.

Mother also had very close relationships with several other men throughout her life, mostly schoolteachers and preachers. She often talked on the phone and exchanged letters with them, gossiping about the politics of their schools or churches. Some of these men almost certainly were gay, but some most certainly were not. She even maintained a lifelong friendship with my very first boyfriend from my pubescent crush days, whom I never actually dated. Chuck looked kind of like Clark Gable, and he charmed the mothers as much as their daughters. In her old age, when Mom started side-swiping cars with her big second-hand Cadillac, Chuck found her a Volvo in which he thought she would be safer. He told her he would change the oil for her and maintain it for her free of charge if she would let him have it when she finally decided to give up driving. A year or so later, when she ran it into a pole, totaling it, Chuck sold it for scrap and gave the money to Mom, who was unhurt in the crash.

For the first 30 years of my life, I shared my mom's bias in favor of males, except for a brief period during childhood when I waged a fierce vendetta against boys, beating them up on the playground every chance I got. The violence started when I entered fourth grade, shortly after the birth of my brother John in 1947. A year earlier, we had moved from the Bible college in Waxachie, Texas, where Dad was dean of men and mother taught piano, to Illinois, where my parents had been called as co-pastors of a tiny church in East St. Louis. It was a move that would have a profoundly negative effect on our whole family. In Texas, my mother had enjoyed an independent income, a job she that made good use of her talents, and an active social life among the faculty. But after the move, although Mom had been called as a co-pastor, the church members treated her like the "pastor's wife," and she made it clear in loud and frequent arguments with Dad that she didn't appreciate playing second fiddle. To make matters worse, she found herself living on the outskirts of a small town without a separate income or a car of her own and with a husband who was often away visiting church members or browsing through second-hand bookstores. When she discovered, at the age of almost 36, that she was pregnant, something must have snapped in her. "Get up off your ass, you lazy hound! I'm the only one who does any work around here!" she would yell at me. When Dad was late for dinner, she loudly accused him of having affairs. And the baby cried with colic every night, promptly at 6 p.m.

Pacing back and forth on the darkened breezeway, holding my baby brother on my shoulder, patting his back and bouncing on the balls of my feet to calm him, I remember whispering in his ear, "Never love your mother" as the tears streamed down my cheeks—a memory that would haunt me with guilt in later years.

Even my dad, whom I adored—and who had always before treated me with love—couldn't contain his frustration. Once, when John stood up and fell out of the high chair on his head, Dad ran into the kitchen yelling, "If you ever let him fall out of that chair again, I'll half kill you!" Another time, when John had spread pots and pans all over the kitchen floor, Dad told me to pick them up. Tired of being my brother's keeper, I shot back, "Pick them up yourself," whereupon Dad began yelling and pulling my hair. Seeing my dad act like that was one of the shocking experiences of my childhood.

We were all more than a little crazy back then.

Only a couple of years before John's birth, boys from the dorm had fetched Dad's golf balls for him as he practiced his drives, and he and Mom had occasionally golfed together, something I don't recall them ever doing again after they took the church in Illinois. With the dormitory cafeteria at our disposal, Mom had almost never cooked, and we all enjoyed attending campus concerts, revival meetings, basketball games and parties hosted by members of the faculty. As icing on the cake, my parents had a whole girls' dormitory full of baby-sitters for me while I reveled in the unofficial post of campus mascot. To this day, I always remember that time in Texas as the best years of my childhood. So our move to Illinois and my brother's birth changed everything for all three of us. (Probably no one will ever know what harm all this did to my infant brother, but that's his story, and one I'm not qualified to tell.)

I'm sure none of us fully understood the dynamics of the situation at the time. For all I knew, I loved my baby brother as if he were my own son. Everyone, including Mom, said I was like a mother to him. I looked after him, rode him on my bike, and even took him on some of my dates. And while I have never ceased to love and cherish him, it didn't dawn on me for many years why I had begun beating up on boys in the fourth grade. By sixth grade, when I made the mistake of picking a fight with some big boys who hadn't been taught to pull their punches with girls, I gave up my active campaign against boys, further repressing what I now realize was a deep resentment of how my brother's birth had coincided with such a total reversal of so many of my childhood pleasures. It is truly amazing what lengths people will go to in order to hide painful realities from themselves.

But despite my unconscious resentment over how my brother's birth had changed my life, for the most part I still preferred the company of males. I wasn't a tomboy, although I did like riding bikes, shooting baskets, and building huts in the woods out of fallen branches; I just thought of boys as somehow better than girls (myself not included) and by the time I was 10 or 11, I was actively pursuing them as boyfriends, running away to marry a "boy" of 20 when I was 14 (a plot that failed) and marrying a "boy" of 26 when I was 19. I put the word in quotes because, while both of these males were considerably older than I, when it came to actively pursuing relations with the opposite sex, I was the more aggressive and confident one—maybe because I had always been a daddy's girl, but perhaps also because my mother's preference for males had exerted more influence on me than I realized. I wanted to be with males, and I wanted them to want to be with me.

It wasn't until shortly after my 30th birthday that I began to question my attitudes about women. In the fall of 1968, I entered Washington University graduate school in St. Louis on a full-tuition scholarship, which could have been extended through to my completion of a Ph.D. in English, providing I could keep up my grades. It was something I had dreamed about for years. But there were immediate complications. During the summer before I entered Wash U, my husband, Harold, had been spending five days a week on the road as press secretary for Paul Simon during his successful run for Lt. Governor of Illinois, leaving me alone to care for the house and the three girls, one of whom had a chronic illness. When the campaign ended, Harold, deciding that politics was not his cup of tea, accepted a job with a newspaper in Dayton, Ohio. So now I had not only to take care of the girls seven days a week while commuting 20 miles each way to school and carrying a full load of graduate work at a university known for rigorous scholarship, but I also had to keep the house in tip-top shape for showing to potential buyers. My only help was a baby-sitter during the hours when I was in class. I will never forget the night I drove straight from my classes in St. Louis to the doctor's office in Illinois to ask for tranquilizers.

Somehow, though, the house got sold, despite the water in the basement, and at the end of the semester, right after Christmas, I surrendered my scholarship so the girls and I could move to Dayton to join their father. I'll never know if giving up that dream of a Ph.D. from an institution I revered contributed to my evolving attitude toward the sexes, but I do remember the exact moment when I became conscious of the change, which was shortly after our move to Dayton.

For the first few months after our move, I found myself with more time on my hands than I had experienced in years. All the girls were in school, and I was neither working nor attending college. Every morning after the everyone had left, I would linger over a second cup of coffee with the newspaper, then get in the car to explore my new city. But even with plenty of books to read and places to explore, I was restless. So I volunteered as a Pink Lady at Good Samaritan Hospital and joined a women's bowling team along with Susie, the one woman I knew in town. Susie's husband had worked with Harold at the newspaper in East St. Louis, and now, through pure coincidence, our husbands were colleagues on the Dayton newspaper. When I walked into the bowling alley that first morning, my immediate reaction was, "Oh, God—all these women!"

And then I heard myself.

After all, I was a woman, I suddenly realized. What did my automatic feeling of revulsion at the sight of so many women say about my self-image? There had been hints that something was amiss before. Once, during a spirited discussion with a football coach and his wife, who were friend of ours, the coach had accused me of thinking I was smarter than my husband. "You're not," he assured me. Since I had always stood in awe of Harold's superior memory, vocabulary, knowledge, and apparent maturity, I was totally thrown off balance by the coach's accusation. I couldn't imagine how he had arrived at that conclusion, and I felt embarrassed and ashamed. And there was another hint that I didn't "know my place": From time to time, when Harold and I had a serious argument, he would accuse me of being a feminist, or some such word. To be perfectly fair, I don't remember the term he used. I just know it seemed to imply that I thought women were as good or better than men, and it always made me feel defensive.

Until, one day, it didn't.

"So what if I AM a feminist?" I asked myself. I had never taken part in any women's marches or become an active spokesperson for women, but I had been reading *Ms. Magazine* and was familiar with the writings of Betty Friedan, Germaine Greer, Simone de Beauvoir, Erica Jong, and others, and apparently their messages were starting to get through to me, because I no longer felt apologetic.

After Harold and I were separated in 1977, I began to develop a genuine appreciation for women. During our separation, which lasted for almost two years, I left teaching to become foundation editor for the Kettering Foundation in Dayton. When I was not working, I spent a lot of time at a local coffee house, reading, playing cards and talking with the owners. Hanging out at the Nite Owl with its colorful clientele helped me forget, momentarily, about the chaotic state of my marriage and family life. Betty, a manicurist several years my junior who worked in the beauty shop above the Nite Owl, was a free spirit who introduced me to partying on a level that I had never experienced as a young housewife and mother. It was the 70s, and the two of us drank wine (I had never tasted alcohol until my late 20s) and ran around with more men than I care to remember, although my fundamentalist background kept me from ever getting drunk or experimenting with drugs, which were readily available among the Nite Owl crowd.

At the same time, I started attending a monthly women's potluck at the home of a woman I had met through Betty. Nadine, a gifted masseuse who operated her business out of the Victorian mansion that was her home, introduced me to several more interesting, intelligent and talented women. That's when I began to realize the unique pleasures of interacting with other women in a male-free environment. When I moved to St. Louis several years later, that first women's potluck provided part of the inspiration for a monthly women's meeting started by my attorney friend, Andrea, that continued for more than 20 years and still has occasional get-togethers. At these meetings, where everyone brings an ingredient for a salad and the hostess provids drinks and dessert, we have shared some of our deepest feelings and most profound experiences, and I have learned to respect and appreciate, at a very basic level, women I might never have come to know in any other context.

Earlier, though, back in Dayton at the Kettering Foundation, I had noticed a woman among the employees who looked as much like a Barbie Doll as a woman could get without plastic surgery: She was tan all year-round with long, shapely legs, slim arched feet tucked into high-heeled shoes, a full bosom, tiny waist, and delicate hands with exquisitely manicured nails. Her clothes were always stylish and wrinkle-free, and there was never a hair out of place. She was friendly to both men and women, but there seemed to be an invisible wall around her. Watching her, I realized that I seldom complimented women on the things I envied about them, so I resolved to form a new habit. Whenever I found anything especially attractive about a woman's appearance or manner, including "Barbie," I would tell her so. As a result, she and I drew closer. She confided that while she had no trouble attracting men, women seemed to keep their distance, which is why she had decided not to lower herself by trying too hard to be friends with them. (Did I mention that her posture was as erect as a ballerina's?) When I left the foundation four years later, she and my secretary, Keta, put together a gala farewell champagne brunch attended by the whole staff, at which speeches were made, toasts were proposed, and everyone had a great time. I will never forget this dear friend's kindness to me.

Meanwhile, my mother, who had divorced my dad after 34 years of marriage, suddenly sold her car, rented out her house, and moved to Paraguay to teach in an interdenominational English language school for children in Asuncion in 1978, a few months before her 67th birthday. Despite the fact that her knowledge of Spanish was rudimentary at best and she didn't know a soul in the whole country, she had a marvelous time there, traveling to tourist sites and neighboring countries with her colleagues and even directing a musical production of "Tom Sawyer" that, if memory serves me well, was performed at the American Embassy. I went to visit Mom in Asuncion and found her happier and more at ease than any time since our days in Waxahachie, Texas, in the 1940s. While I was there, she confessed that, still suffering from deep depression brought on when my dad married one of her best friends a couple of years after their divorce, she had made the decision to go to Paraguay as a kind of symbolic suicide. "I thought I would go as far away as I could get, where nobody knew me and I didn't know anyone, and just die," she said. But life had other plans. Eventually, when her sister died unexpectedly, she rushed back to the arms of her family in the United States, unable to shake a guilty feeling that she had abandoned them all to pursue her own selfish ends. But for several years afterwards, her colleagues and students at the school continued to urge her to return.

Although Mom decided not to go back to Asuncion, she had tasted freedom, just as she had in her early years as a traveling musician and woman preacher, and she had liked the taste of it. One of the profound lessons I took from seeing how happy she was in Paraguay was that the best thing a woman can do for her children is to make herself happy, because it relieves them from the burden of worrying about a parent. Although I have tried to follow my own advice in that regard, I confess that I haven't been as successful as I would like, but I keep trying.

Upon her return from Paraguay, Mom embarked on a research project to document the history of women ministers in the Assemblies of God movement—a project that kept her busy for five years and resulted in a book (self-published), which I edited for her, called *Behold God's Handmaid, by Mary Ruth Chamless, 1988*. Through her own efforts and those of the Gospel Publishing House in Springfield, Missouri, Mom sold more than 1,000 copies of her book before she died in 2003.

In one way or another, life keeps changing, and so do we. So despite a lingering sadness and regret that my dreams of a happy marriage and united family did not last a lifetime, my experiences during the 30-plus years since my separation and divorce from the father of my children have included an ever-growing appreciation for women. I am thankful for a wealth of deep and enduring relationships with women, including my three daughters, that have helped me through the hard times, supported my efforts, and encouraged me never to give up on my goals. I hope I have done the same for them.

As I think back over what I have written, I remember reading my Grandma Ruth (Schafer) Rainbolt's valedictory speech to her high school graduating class, which was more literate and articulate than most of the essays from college freshmen that I have read as a teacher. She married at 19 and bore eight children over the course of 22 years. Grandpa Rainbolt, a carpenter, moved the family around a lot, following the jobs, and my mother told me more than once that her mother could move the whole household in a day and still have dinner on the table in the new house promptly at five o'clock. A classic matriarch who was generous to a fault, Grandma Rainbolt made clothes for everyone and often exasperated her children by passing on to others the presents they had given her when she found someone she thought needed them more. She helped her children in many ways, but she also meddled in their personal lives and marriages perhaps more than was appropriate. Looking back, I suspect that, while running a home and raising eight children is no piece of cake, those tasks didn't provide enough outlets for her high intelligence and energy.

My other grandmother, Etta Julia (Thurman) Chamless, did not marry until 28, after which she bore 11 children in the next 15 years with her preacher husband, who, she told me, didn't believe in birth control. Born in Texas when it was still a very wild and rough place, she said that, as a toddler, she had been a passenger in a wagon in the famous Oklahoma Run (a fact that my brother, the family genealogist, has so far been unable to confirm). Legend also has it that she led a very colorful life before her marriage to the preacher, having been the mistress of a gambling man and nursemaid to Joan Crawford. Despite her lack of education and life of poverty as a preacher's wife, she was remarkably progressive in her thinking. In a family photograph from the early days of her marriage, instead of standing stiffly behind her husband as women usually did in such photographs, she is leaning one elbow on her husband's shoulder and resting her head on a finger lightly touching her chin, an impish gleam in her eye. She told me one time that when she started menstruating, she was terrified because no one had ever told her the facts of life, so she made up her mind that she would educate her children early in life about such things, and she did, several generations before sex education became popular in the schools. After she divorced my grandpa, she managed to support herself for another 30 years or so by running a boarding house, and although she had no money to leave to her children, I believe she passed on to them something more valuable: a creative and entrepreneurial spirit that produced a wide variety of professionals among her descendants.

While I believe that being a good parent—if one is a parent—is more important than anything else one can do, I find it interesting to ponder what more my grandmothers might have accomplished had they lived in times where effective birth control was available and women were free to pursue careers outside the home.

Although I still like men very much, today it saddens me when I hear women make demeaning or derogatory generalizations about their gender, and I am bothered by surveys showing that women are still more competitive with, and less tolerant of, other women in the workplace. These attitudes, I believe, have the power of self-fulfilling prophecy. I don't know how much of the lingering competition between women is Darwinian in nature, as some people claim, arising out of a drive to capture the best possible male for breeding, but I am convinced that it is self-destructive, and I'm grateful for the many wonderful, close, supportive friendships I have been privileged to forge with women in the second half of my life.

Perhaps the greatest personal benefit from my changed attitude, though, is that it has helped me to understand and appreciate my mother in ways that I had never been able to do when I was younger. As a highly talented, intelligent, independent-spirited woman, she was trapped in a world that did not fully recognize her talents or encourage her to see how far she could go. She was angry and frustrated without knowing exactly why, and she sometimes lashed out at those closest to her. But I'm convinced that something in her spirit, which was passed on through me to her granddaughters, has helped them to forge new paths for women in today's world.

Pets

I thought I was a dog person until I met Daisy. The only pet I ever had when I was growing up was a dog, and I didn't have him for long. Grandpa Rainbolt, who was a foreman for a construction company, found him on a job site and brought him home to me when I was so young I can barely remember it. That must have been during one of the years when we were living in Illinois in the summer and Texas in the winter, or perhaps the first year after we moved to Illinois for good, when I was going on eight years old. The dog was such a lively little thing that I named him Jitterbug—"Jitter," for short—after the dance that was currently all the rage. I don't even remember for sure what color he was, although I think he was black and white. I do remember that Daddy taught him to jump over a stick, much to my delight. In my mind's eye, I see Daddy in the kitchen, holding a broom handle for Jitter to jump as Daddy raised it ever higher, but I'm sure the dog wasn't allowed to stay in the house overnight. Mom, who was very germ-conscious, didn't allow animals to live in the house.

As too often happens to animals who live outdoors and are not fenced in, Jitter didn't enjoy a long life. He was found dead in the woods near our house just a few weeks after I got him—either killed by a wild animal or by a pack of dogs who had previously ganged up on a neighbor's Pekingese. I always thought they were jealous of the Pekingese because it was pampered by the owner, and perhaps they had the same instinct about Jitter because we were so fond of him. I know I must have been very sad about losing him—perhaps so sad that

I repressed the memory, since I can't recall the feeling. In any case, I never had another pet while I was growing up.

Mom didn't hate animals. She showed compassion for them if they were in distress, and she said she and Dad had a dog named Penny and a cat named Nickel when they were first married. She told me when Dad would go out hunting for rabbits for food, the cat would follow him like a hound dog, with his tail straight up in the air. But I think she thought it was unnatural for people and animals to live together indoors. And she was especially averse to having cats in the house. More than once she told me with a shudder about having seen a cat up on someone's table drinking out of the family milk jug when she was a child. So I was never encouraged to have pets.

After I was married to Harold Piety, our family had several animals over the years, including dogs, cats, a toad that wouldn't eat anything but live flies that Harold had to stun with a swatter, a field mouse who ran himself to death in a hamster wheel, a large tortoise named "Myrtle the Turtle" who lived in the basement and went with the girls for Show and Tell, and a fish my middle daughter, Titi, named "Mom"— probably because it was always opening its mouth. When the fish died, I thought Titi took a rather unseemly glee in announcing to all and sundry that "Mom died."

Even though we had a lot of pets, however, I didn't think of any of them as particularly mine. They belonged to the family. Jill, the dog we had when we separated, was definitely Harold's. When he would come home from work at night, Jill would rush to the door to greet him, running in circles and wagging her tail wildly as Harold loudly exclaimed, "Hello, little black dog!" After dinner, when Harold went in to lie on the living room floor to listen to Beethoven symphonies on the record player, Jill was usually nestled up beside him, the picture of contentment. But at night, when the other family members had gone to bed, I would sometimes sit by Jill's bed and talk to her. I felt a kinship with her because she was afraid of lots of things, and so was I.

One of the things that terrified Jill was the meter man's loud banging on the back door near her bed. He always yelled "Meter man!" at the top of his lungs, probably to make sure people controlled their dogs and that nobody shot him for an intruder. Although we all loved our beautiful Dayton View neighborhood in Ohio with its charming and gracious houses, it *was* in the city, in "transition" during the early 1970s, and experiencing a pretty high level of violence, so perhaps the meter man felt one couldn't be too careful. In any case, I would quietly commiserate with Jill when no one was around. I felt a strong kinship with her and all of my fellow creatures who were plagued by fears of the unknown and felt pushed around by forces they couldn't always control or understand. But Jill was still the family dog, and mainly Harold's.

Our first cat, and the only cat that we had for long, was Miss Kitty, a coal-black, beautiful, fluffy cat of indeterminate origin who seemed to have wandered into our lives quite by accident. Although she lived in the house, she went in and out, and somehow she managed to get herself knocked up shortly after she adopted us. Harold established a birthing room for her in a cloth-lined box right next to the huge old gravity furnace in the basement, and at the appointed time she gave birth to several darling little kittens. Too darling, apparently, because soon they all disappeared. After a thorough search of the house— all three stories and the basement—we finally found the kittens in Harold's closet, in one of his shirt boxes from the laundry. The only possible conclusion was that Miss Kitty had carried them, one-by-one, up two flights of stairs, to hide them from all the humans who had been making too much of a fuss over them. I would like to say that Miss Kitty taught me a lesson about mothering, because while she was fiercely protective of her babies as kittens, once they were grown, she treated them just like any other cats. Although I admired her ability to detach and let go of her grown-up offspring, it wasn't a lesson I found easy to emulate.

After the kittens were born, we resolved to get Miss Kitty spayed as soon as possible to avoid any more "accidents," but once again she contrived to outsmart us. We had tried to keep her in the house, away from prowling toms, until the kittens were weaned and she could be fixed, but, as cats will do, she managed to slip out the door once, and once was all it took: When Harold brought her home from the vet's, he announced with a sad face that she had been found to be carrying six tiny kittens in her womb. It was obvious that he felt like a party to abortion. Harold always did love babies.

Despite how cute they were, as the first batch of kittens grew up, we gradually unloaded them on friends and family. Eldridge Cleaver, the one we kept the longest, was a lively little coal-black short-haired cat who had a special place in our hearts. Once my middle daughter, Titi, caught him standing on a dining room chair, carefully scraping leftovers off of a plate to Jill, who was waiting below to catch them. We eventually gave Eldridge Cleaver to my dad and stepmother in Illinois and were sad to hear, sometime later, that he had suffered a fate similar to that of my little dog Jitter, apparently attacked by a wild animal in the wooded area around Dad's house.

Although I loved all of these animals, they were family pets; I never thought of them as exclusively mine. When Harold moved to

Chicago after our separation, he took Jill with him, and, having had my consciousness raised about all living creatures in the years since then, I'm ashamed to admit that I don't remember how or when we lost Miss Kitty.

My second husband, Evan, had two cats—Cymru and Ddraig (Evan was of Welsh descent). They were cute and clever—Ddraig knew how to climb up into the pantry and open the Tender Vittles, and once we came home to find him lying, drunk as a skunk, in the middle of a pile of catnip he had removed from its bag in the pantry, a silly smile on his face and his tail lazily swaying to and fro. But they were definitely Evan's cats. They had been his long before he met me, and they were with him several years after we parted. In fact, if I had to say whom he loved best—the cats or me—I'm convinced the cats would have won, hands down.

During the years after my second divorce, while I held various writing and editing jobs in three states, I never considered having a pet. For one thing, some of my jobs were very demanding and time-consuming, and for another, I loved to travel and run around at night, so I thought it would be cruel to leave an animal at home alone so much.

Shortly after I retired and moved to a 100-year-old house on a huge, tree-shaded lot in Stillwater, Oklahoma, though, fate brought a pet to me. My daughter Tamara, who had been offered a chance to teach law in London for five months, asked if I would care for her dog, Bubba, while she was gone. The truth is that I was still a little frightened of larger dogs, and Bubba, a thick-coated, stray, good ole boy from Arkansas who looked like a chubby shepherd/heeler mix, was a little intimidating, but he turned out to be a sweetheart, sleeping beside my bed at night and making me feel safer in my new home, even though he did give me a temporary case of arthritis in the fingers of my right hand from pulling on the leash so hard when I took him for his daily walks. So when Tamara returned from England and I had to give him back, I began to think about getting a pet of my very own. Perhaps unconsciously I was still remembering my mother's revulsion at seeing the cat up on the table drinking from the family's milk jug, or maybe it was because I had come to love my granddog, Bubba, but I assumed that if I got a pet, it would be a dog.

Until I met Daisy.

I know it's a cliché, but it really was a case of love at first sight. I was visiting Judy, my daughter Julia's sister-in-law, on her farm outside Stillwater when a fluffy little black-and-white kitten with a Phantom of the Opera face came up and rested her paws on Judy's leg, looking up at her as if to speak. "Her name should be Daisy," the thought popped into my head, totally apropos of nothing. I had never known anyone, animal or human, named Daisy, except in the "Dagwood" cartoon, and that Daisy was a dog who didn't look anything like this charming little kitten. When I commented on how cute she was, Judy, who was used to having lots of stray cats running around the farm, said, "I think someone must have dropped her off out here because she acts more tame than the other cats. I put a litter box up on the back porch for her and she uses it, and she sleeps in the bed I made for her there. Would you like to take her home with you?"

Taken off guard, I could only respond, "I'll think about it." When I got home that night, I called Julia and told her what had happened. Julia, a self-proclaimed "crazy cat lady" and lover of all creatures great and small, responded, "You know, when you give an animal a name, that means it belongs to you." I thought a lot about that because it seemed really strange that her name had suddenly popped into my mind like that, but I still wasn't convinced that I was a cat person. And I was still uncertain a week or so later when Judy called me to ask, "Have you given any more thought to taking that kitten?" As a matter of fact, I had, so I agreed to take her home with me on a trial basis. I'm not sure which of us it was more of a trial for, but I know it wasn't entirely easy for Daisy.

For one thing, she wouldn't stay off the kitchen table. I had inherited a lot of my mother's squeamishness about germs—I would never think, for example, of eating from another person's fork—so I was determined to teach Daisy to stay off the table. "Man makes plans and God laughs," the saying goes. I suspect that saying could have originated with the early Egyptian cat worshippers, because I quickly learned that once a cat has made up its mind to do something you have forbidden it to do, you either have to get rid of the cat or adapt to change. I tried all kinds of tactics—yelling at her, spraying her with water, swatting her with a rolled-up newspaper, even roughly knocking her off the table with a sweep of my arm—but the harder I tried, the more determined she seemed to be. She would be back up there before I took the next breath. Finally, I took the extreme measure of hitting her with a yardstick, something she made sure that I would never forget.

After being hit with the yardstick, she stayed off the table and, thinking I had won, I sat down to grade papers from the freshman composition class I was teaching at Oklahoma State University. Just to be sure she didn't try anything again, though, I laid the yardstick on the table beside me, part of it hanging off the side so I could grab it quickly, if necessary. Slowly, and with great dignity, Daisy stood erect on her hind legs and carefully examined the yardstick with her front paws, as if to say, "So this is the instrument you tortured me with." I was instantly assailed by the world-famous image of the lone Chinese student bravely defying the tanks in Tiananmen Square, and I was ashamed.

My daughter Titi, the philosophy professor and a cat lover herself, added another dimension to my understanding of Daisy's position on this issue. "Cats are territorial animals," she explained to me. "So from Daisy's point of view, the house and yard are hers, and she is allowing you to live in them." Oh.

After the incident of the yardstick, I have never tried to keep Daisy off the table again, except when I have dinner guests, when I shut her in the study. (I eat most of my solitary meals from a TV tray, where there is not room for her.) And perhaps as a gesture of goodwill, she has never—well, hardly ever—let me catch her exploring the kitchen countertops. While I was baking bread or engaged in other complex cooking tasks at the little house in Stillwater, she would sit on the table in the middle of the kitchen to watch me work, reminding me of myself as a little girl, when I had loved to hang around the neighbor ladies' kitchens, chatting them up and watching them do their chores.

The house in Stillwater had a huge yard—130 ft. x 150 ft.—with lots of tall trees and shrubs, so there was always plenty of yard work for me to do and Daisy liked to follow me around when I was working. The street in front of the house was rather busy, and once, soon after I got her, she started running toward it. Terrified that she would be hit by a car, I screamed "Daisy!" and—like a cartoon character, I swear—she came to a screeching halt before reaching the street. We lived there together for four years, and she never tried to cross the street again. Since she was used to living outdoors, I let her wander outside when I was home, but she stuck to our side of the street and mainly stayed in our own yard, eventually coming whenever I called her. I still recall with fondness seeing her strolling across the lawn toward me from the thicket in the back corner of the yard that I liked to think of as my "little woods." Sometimes we would sit together on the bench under the big oak tree, and sometimes she would rock with me in the swing that hung on the porch that ran the length of the east side of the house. At night, as she slept in the bed beside me, I would look at my mother's photograph over the bed and wonder if she was rolling over in her grave at the thought of me sleeping with a cat. But I have a theory that, after people are dead, if they are still spirits, they are able to put things into better perspective, so I don't think she would be worrying about it.

The little house in Oklahoma was a paradise for me and Daisy during the years that we lived there, but when I found that I was able to indulge my love of travel after retirement more than I had anticipated, I felt kind of bad about leaving her at home all alone, even though I found a couple of really great cat sitters—Cameron and Charissa—who took turns coming in and caring for her when I was away. Still, I thought she must get lonesome, so I decided to get a companion for her.

Since the farm where I had acquired Daisy always had plenty of cats, that seemed the logical place to go for another one, and I decided that, this time, I would get an all-black male cat. Actually, upon reflection, I'm not sure I was the one who decided. When I went back to Judy's farm, there was one little black kitten who always seemed glad to let me pet him, unlike the others, who usually shied away from human contact, so it made sense to pick him. When I came back to the farm with a cat carrier, it took less than a minute for me to get him into it and on the way home again. I would later decide that Felix had been asking me to rescue him, but for a few weeks, it looked as if he had gone from a bad situation to a horrible one.

For one thing, Daisy clearly didn't appreciate my humanitarian gesture of bringing her a companion. As soon as she saw him, she began hissing and growling like a wild thing; I had to keep him shut up in the bedroom with his food, water and litter box during the day, so she could get used to having him around without killing him. At night, she would take her place on the bed beside me and make it clear to both of us that he was not welcome, so he had to slink off to the living room to sleep alone.

For another, I discovered when I took Felix to the vet that he was not a kitten, after all. "He has an adult set of teeth," she told me. Apparently, he had simply been undernourished. Ear mites, worms, and some scars on his body suggested that life on the farm had not been a piece of cake for the poor little boy.

And then there was the matter of castration. For a small cat (seven pounds when I got him), he had a rather impressive set of cajones, and having them rudely cut off only added one more level of trauma to what he had probably first envisioned as a blissful rescue but had discovered to be a nightmare. The next thing I knew, his hair started falling out.

After several tests, during which time Felix became almost totally bald, the vet finally decided he had some kind of mites and prescribed a series of dips for both Daisy and Felix, which they hated and feared, and which didn't seem to be doing Felix the least bit of good. That's when I decided to make an unscientific diagnosis and prescribe my own unconventional cure. "He's simply having a severe anxiety attack," I decided, being uncomfortably familiar with anxiety attacks myself. So I cancelled the final appointment for de-nitting dips and prescribed some additional TLC and a diet of cottage cheese for the ailing kitty, who had also been suffering from bouts of diarrhea. I remembered that when one of our dogs had a similar problem, the vet had suggested that we feed him cottage cheese and it had worked, so over the course of a couple of weeks, I fed Felix about two cartons of cottage cheese. He ate it up, and his hair started to grow back. Now he has a beautifully shiny black coat, but he has never shown any interest in cottage cheese since. Just call me Dr. Piety.

Before his ordeal came to an end, however, we discovered that Felix had one more problem. As I mentioned, Daisy would not allow him up on the bed at night, but one time I awoke in the middle of the night to find him nestled between us, feverishly hot, his breathing loud and rough. It was obvious that his condition was dire enough to cause him to brave Daisy's wrath, and perhaps she recognized the gravity of the situation, because she hadn't run him off. Luckily, the Oklahoma State University veterinary school clinic was only a few blocks away and open all night. Their tests and x-rays revealed that Felix had a lung infection, for which he had to take steroids and antibiotics. His lung problem has cropped up two or three times since, and the vet and I have concluded that he has asthma. Now whenever he starts that raspy breathing once every month or two, one prednisone pill seems to stop it in its tracks. I'm estimating that he is eight years old now, and still lively, jumping from the back of the settee to my stomach so hard when I am lying down that I have taken to covering myself with a bolster when I take a nap, to protect myself from a ruptured spleen. So I believe when I took him from the farm, I saved his life. And glad I am that I did, since he is the most loving, gentle cat (aside from the jumping) that anyone could ever want.

Over the past four years, Daisy and Felix have had to undergo a lot of change. Between 2009 and 2013, we moved five times: first, temporarily, to my friend George's house in St. Louis, to see if I wanted to actually sell my house in Oklahoma and move back to the city; then back to live in the house for the summer and get it ready for sale; then to an apartment across from the Missouri Botanical Garden in St. Louis; then to my friend Pam's house, when the ceiling over the bathtub in my apartment collapsed in the middle of the night; and, finally, to an apartment across from Tilles Park in St. Louis, which I like very much and in which I sincerely hope to stay until I have to be carted off to the nursing home or to St. Louis University hospital, where I have arranged in advance to donate my body. Daisy and Felix have been excellent travelers through all this, riding between Oklahoma and St. Louis three times. They cried piteously for a couple of nights in our first two moves, but I discovered some collars impregnated with mama-cat pheromones that made the more recent moves a lot less stressful.

The worst problem for Daisy is that she can no longer roam free outside during the day because the management won't allow it. My daughter Julia thinks that's a good thing, since she says cats are safer and live longer when they're not allowed to roam, but I feel sorry for

Daisy because I remember how much I loved to be out in the fields when I was a girl. So I am trying to make things easier for her: I have bought a "Kitty Holster" and on good-weather days I take her outside on a leash, or I hook her to a long line attached to a stake and sit in a lawn chair and read while she explores the flowers and shrubs and watches the squirrels shimmy up the trees. She still begs to go outside fairly often, but she seems to be getting used to the leash.

In my declining years, I don't feel much romantic interest in men my age, and I don't want to embarrass myself by going after young ones, so Daisy and Felix provide me with the physical affection and loving companionship without which I most certainly could not survive. Warm, soft and cuddly, they are always available for hugs and sweet talk, and they don't care how old I am or what I look like. Although I love them both dearly, my love is different for each of them: With Felix I feel very maternal, while my attitude toward Daisy might more accurately be described as worshipful. In any case, they are my best friends, and I am most fortunate to have them. I read in one of Julia's books that the oldest cat on record lived to be 34, and I know of several people whose cats have lived for 20 years, so I'm hoping to have both of them around for the rest of my life.

Ice Cream

As I wander back through the long hallways of memory in search of the origin of my love affair with ice cream, the first picture that comes to mind is a dime store on the corner of Broadway and Washington in St. Louis that made ice cream sandwiches out of freshly baked waffles and little rectangular slabs of ice cream that came wrapped in white paper. My mother and I used to stop there on our infrequent shopping trips to the city from our home across the Mississippi River in Illinois during the 1940s. I'm no longer sure whether the store was a Kresge's or Woolworth's—or even if I have the intersection right, since everything has changed so much—but the tantalizing smell of fresh-baked waffles that permeated the store and the delicious first taste of vanilla ice cream encased in warm, crisp waffles are as real to me now as they were some 70 years ago.

The second memory that pops up in my internal word association game is not a happy one and not really about ice cream at all, but about my little brother, John, who was born in July 1947, a little over a year after our family made the permanent move from our winter home at the Southwestern Bible Institute in Waxahachie, Texas, to live year-round in Collinsville, Illinois. Before John's birth, I had been an only child for nearly nine years and something of a rock star, having been first the pastors' baby girl, next the traveling evangelists' performing daughter, and most recently the unofficial campus mascot at Southwestern Bible Institute in Waxahachie before my abrupt promotion to Big Sister. In what I now regard as a spectacularly successful Freudian effort at sublimating any trace of sibling rivalry, I almost instantly transformed myself into John's other ("real") mom, watching over him at least as tenderly as our biological mother. When John was just learning to walk, several people from our church were enjoying an ice cream social at a member's house on a lazy summer afternoon, with various folks taking turns at hand-cranking the ice cream maker, when John slipped while trying to rise to his feet with the help of a coffee table and fell backward on the padded carpet. It was the kind of fall that toddlers take every day—nothing to get excited about—except that on this occasion my brother turned blue and passed out. Without stopping to call an ambulance, my parents grabbed him, climbed into a car driven by a parishioner and headed straight to the hospital, about five miles away. During the eternity in which all of us back at the house waited for news, I begged God to save my baby brother and wondered if my parents had forgotten all about me. When the call finally came, we learned that John had remained unconscious for approximately 40 minutes. Although he appeared to be fine when he came to, he had to stay overnight in the hospital, where he was awakened once an hour to ensure that he had not lapsed into a coma. I don't know how I got home that night. I just remember the overwhelming fear, loneliness and helplessness in the face of unanticipated disaster that flooded me then and has recurred periodically throughout my life.

The majority of my ice cream memories are happy ones, though. Each summer that my parents pastored the church in East St. Louis (from my third-grade through 10th-grade years), the church hosted a 4th of July picnic at one of two large parks, Grand Marais (later Frank Holten) State Park and Jones Park, operated by the city. An all-day affair, the 4th of July picnic was filled with men's softball games, women sitting around chatting amiably and children running through the grass playing all the games that children played back then: hide-and-seek, "Mother, may I?", dodgeball, tag, croquet, badminton, and softball. For that one annual occasion, my mother would sew us matching mother-and-daughter playsuits, consisting of a one-piece overall-type garment with shorts on the bottom half, covered by a skirt that buttoned around the waist. Of course we never took off the skirts—that would have been unthinkable among our Pentecostal church members—but it was still fun to get to wear shorts, which I was never allowed to do after the age of nine. The meal was potluck, liberally supplemented by church-supplied hot dogs and hamburgers on the grill, soda pop, and ice cream treats in a large box filled with dry ice, which gave off a white smoke and burned our hands when we children tried to play with it, which, of course, we always did.

So ice cream and I go way back. But it isn't just the dessert itself that holds a special appeal for me; it's the whole nostalgic ambiance of ice cream parlors. I think maybe the source of my lifelong affection for them began at a combination sandwich shop/soda fountain on Main Street in Collinsville called "The Greeks'" because it was owned by the Karnages, a Greek family in our neighborhood whose children, Georgia and Jimmy, were the objects of my adoration because of their dark good looks. I suspect that's where I tasted my first ice cream soda, and I have never been able to resist the lure of an ice cream parlor since—especially if it features wire-backed chairs and marble-topped tables like The Greeks'. And if it boasts a person behind the counter who knows how to make chocolate ice cream sodas, I am, for the time it takes to enjoy one, completely in heaven.

So you can imagine how fortuitous it was that the man I married at 19 was a former soda jerk and one of the rapidly diminishing number of people on earth who knew the proper way to make a chocolate ice cream soda! That wasn't the reason I married him, of course, but it seemed like an auspicious sign. We had known each other only five months when we married, and I had not met any of the members of his family before the wedding, so after our marriage, when he started talking in his sleep, I listened very carefully, hoping to find out more about this fascinating man of mystery. During one of the first months of our marriage, he sat up in bed at about 2 a.m. and started putting on his shoes and socks. "Where are you going?" I asked, assuming that he mistakenly thought he had heard the alarm clock, since he usually had to get up before dawn to go to work at the newspaper, where he was a sportswriter. Ignoring my question, he continued wordlessly to get dressed in the dark. About the third time I asked him what he was doing, he exclaimed in exasperation, "Pat, I'm going to get up, put on my shoes, and go under the sink and make some salicylic acid!" a declaration that sounded disturbingly sinister at the time. Later, when I told him what he had said, he explained that salicylic acid, a basic ingredient of aspirin, is also used somehow in the process of making ice cream. Apparently, in his dreams, he had wandered back to his soda jerk days.

I guess Harold enjoyed that time in his life, because he liked ice cream a lot, too. When the kids were small and we were still living in Illinois, we used to take them to the movies at the Lincoln Theater in Belleville, stopping first at the Lincoln Soda Shop next door for sandwiches and ice cream treats. (I'm not sure that was its real name, but that's what we always called it.) After we moved to Dayton, Ohio, we got an electric ice-cream maker and Harold often made ice cream for the whole family. He preferred using Jersey milk, with its high fat content, and we were fortunate to live only a few miles from Young's Dairy, a farm near Yellow Springs which sold Jersey milk and ice cream. So after a delightful ride in the Ohio countryside to Young's Dairy, we would return home to await Harold's homemade ice cream. It was hard to improve on the basic product, but he sometimes added strawberries or raspberries from his garden. I wonder if any of us realized then what a heaven we were privileged to inhabit?

Once when our oldest daughter was just entering her teens, our family took a four-week road trip to California to visit Harold's Dad in Paradise. (When he retired and moved from San Francisco, Grandpa Piety took an impish delight in informing us that, from now on, we would have to visit him in Paradise.) We loaded our green Pontiac station wagon with a heavy canvas tent and camped out at KOA and Safari campgrounds along the Interstate whenever we could. After visiting Grandpa on his little "farm," we drove on up to spend a couple of nights each in Lassen Volcanic Park and Crater Lake, Oregon, taking the coastal highway all the way up to Seattle. In Bellevue, Washington, we discovered an old-fashioned ice cream parlor called the Early Dawn Ice Creamery. It was a vision in pink, offering 36 flavors of ice cream and various special treats, including banana splits ($1.09) and ice cream sodas (60 cents). While I'm not sure the girls would even remember the place, since we had many other great experiences on that trip, it was one of the highlights for me. I still have the pink menu in the photo album I made of the trip, which is how I know what everything cost.

A few years after we moved to Dayton, a Friendly's restaurant opened up, pushing my ice cream obsession into high gear. If you're from the East Coast—especially around Boston—you probably know all about Friendly's, which features ice cream, along with great sandwiches, soups and salads. So now, in addition to going to Cassano's for pizza once a week, our family made frequent trips to Friendly's. In fact, we were there so often that the waitresses learned our orders by heart. Like me, Harold usually ordered a chocolate ice cream soda, but unlike me, he was always careful to ask the waitress, "And would you put the ice cream in the glass, please?" You see, instead of topping their sodas with whipped cream, like most places do, Friendly's had a little trick of hanging a scoop of ice cream on the side of the glass, and when you tipped it into the glass, the chemical reaction between the sparkling soda water and the milky ice cream would create a bubbling burst of foam that would inevitably cause the glass to overflow. Harold, who had a lot of ideas about the proper way to do things, thought this didn't make sense, and he politely but firmly let them know it each time he ordered. One day, he threw the waitress a curve by ordering a hot fudge sundae. Without pausing to think, the waitress responded, "And would you like that ice cream in the glass, sir?" All of us, including the waitress, had a good laugh at that.

When the girls were teenagers, Friendly's became one of my two major means of escape from the growing chaos at home. We lived next door to two sisters, Josephine and Hermene Schwarz, founders of the prestigious Dayton Ballet Company and the Dayton School of Ballet, and our eldest daughter, Tamara, was an eager student at their school, as well as an aspiring member of the company, so we sometimes took in boarders who came to study at the school during the summer. Once, we even boarded a dancer for a whole school year. We affectionately dubbed her Annie Fannie, after the cartoon character in *Playboy Magazine*, but sometimes my affection for her was stretched to its limits. A dancer since early childhood, Annie Fannie had lived in other people's homes, traveling from ballet school to ballet school for a good part of her life and apparently missing out on some of the social training that most children get in a stable family setting. She usually declined to sit down to dinner with us, claiming that she wasn't hungry (dancers survive mainly on yogurt, diet soda and air, it seems), but later she would come into the kitchen and stick her finger in the peanut butter jar to grab a bite or open a can of tuna. I felt sorry for her but guilty that I couldn't like her more. One very cold and snowy day during Annie Fannie's stay with us, after having been kept awake half the night by the loud music coming from the stereo downstairs directly beneath our bedroom, I decided I couldn't take it any more.

Bundling myself in boots and the warmest clothes I could find, I grabbed a book and headed out the door, plowing through the deep snow. I had no idea where I was going, but I was determined to find some peace and quiet. Sometime later I found myself sitting in the cozy environment of a Wendy's, about a mile and a half from home, drinking a Diet Pepsi and quietly reading a novel. I felt so invigorated upon my return that I began taking daily walks—often to Wendy's, but sometimes to other places. Sometimes I would even ride the bus to another part of town and walk home, and once I rode it to Children's Hospital, where I sat in the waiting room and read. In those pre-cell-phone days, I liked the idea that nobody knew where I was. Friendly's soon became my other escape hatch. "I'm going to the grocery store," I would announce to the girls while heading out the door, grocery list in hand and novel discreetly tucked under my elbow, failing to mention that I intended to stop off at Friendly's on the way to enjoy an ice cream soda and some quiet reading time. It was what my Sunday School teacher probably would have labeled a "lie of omission," and my conscience did bother me a bit about it—but not enough to make me stop.

In the late 1970s, after Harold and I had divorced and the girls had all left home for college, my ice cream jones experienced a hiatus of several years when I moved to Phoenix, Arizona, at the age of 45 to start a new life with a second husband. Despite the fact that my second marriage ended quickly and Phoenix didn't appear to have a single ice cream parlor, I stayed on there for more than five years, working for American Express. It's just as well that I didn't have much access to my favorite treat, since a couple of years after my second divorce, I fell madly in love with an Olympic athlete who was young enough to be my son, which triggered a vigorous regimen of dieting and workouts that resulted in my losing 20 pounds, developing some pretty impressive abs, and getting my body fat down to about 17 percent.

My physical condition immediately started to deteriorate, however, when, at the age of 50, I quit my job in Phoenix and moved to St. Louis to be near my aging and ailing parents. Soon after my arrival, while attending the First Unitarian Church of St. Louis, I found a friend named George Stair who introduced me to an ideal place to indulge my passion. According to *Wikipedia*, Crown Candy Kitchen, on St. Louis Avenue in Old North St. Louis, "was founded in 1913 by two Macedonian immigrants, and is still run by the three grandsons of Harry Karandzieff, Andy, Tommy, and Mike. This Saint Louis landmark is the oldest operating soda fountains in the metro area, and one of the oldest in the country." With its battered white wooden booths, juke box, and Coca-Cola trays adorning the walls, it is virtually unchanged from the time it was restored after being damaged by a fire several decades ago. Recently, the restaurant has achieved national fame and has been spotlighted on TV, radio, magazines, and the Internet, but when George and I first started going there, it was an uncrowded early-evening refuge for delicious old-fashioned ice cream sodas and quiet conversation. Often, when I got a sudden urge for ice cream, George would respond to my last-minute phone calls like a good sport and swing by my apartment to pick me up, which is one reason, although not the only one by any means, that he has been one of my best friends for nearly 25 years.

Crown Candy Kitchen had always been a popular spot for lunch for the downtown working crowd during the day, as well as a favorite hangout for firemen and police officers, but its location in a rather dark, run-down, half-abandoned old neighborhood tended to scare away the evening clientele, so most times our only company around 9 p.m. was a couple of cops who liked to hang out there and chat with the owners during their patrol of the neighborhood. In the past five years, an abandoned open-air shopping mall across the street has been restored and re-opened, and the neighborhood has been spruced up a bit. These changes, plus all the publicity, have made the place an extremely popular establishment. If you try to go there during the day now, you have to stand in a long line and the place is crowded and noisy, but what's worse is they have cut back their evening hours. They still make a great ice cream soda, so I occasionally try to catch them in the late afternoon, when the crowds have subsided, but it's just as well that I'm not going so often anymore; I've already had way too many of their famous "heart-stopping BLT sandwiches," loaded with enough bacon for four sandwiches and accompanied by potato chips. The sleek, muscular me of the 1980s is long gone, thanks in part to Crown Candy Kitchen.

After my retirement and move to Oklahoma in 2003, I discovered another favorite of ice cream lovers throughout that state and downstate Missouri: Braum's restaurants. Although their stores lack the ambience of a true ice cream parlor, they have great ice cream, and it's inexpensive. During my five years in Stillwater before moving back to St. Louis, I spent many a happy hour at Braum's—with my dear Oklahoma friends or sitting alone, reading a book and sipping a soda, and when I go back for visits, I try to make at least one stop there. On a recent Christmas, when I visited my daughter Julia in Enid, her husband, Phill, gave me a rather large gift certificate for Braum's, which I used while driving back and forth to the state. He couldn't have given me a better present.

Now that I'm back in St. Louis, George and I often go to another favorite St. Louis hangout, Ted Drewes, where the crowds look daunting but the lines move with incredible speed, and literally scores of people stand around outside or lean on cars in the parking lot on hot, muggy St. Louis evenings enjoying the informal party spirit as much as the "ice cream." I put "ice cream" in quotes because Ted Drewes is a custard stand, where no one would know how to make an ice cream soda even if they had the ingredients. The closest I can come to getting a soda there is to order a root beer float, which isn't bad, but it isn't the same, either.

But, then, nothing ever really stays the same over time, does it? Only through the great gift of memory can we have it all.

Fine Dining and Greasy Spoons

I wasn't born with a silver spoon in my mouth. My mother's family was blue-collar poor during the Great Depression, and my daddy's family was even poorer. By the time I came along, on Oct. 7, 1938, my parents were pastoring a little church in Highlands, Texas, and living on whatever was put in the offering plate on Sunday morning by the church members, who were mostly poor, too. So instead of money, people often gave us produce from their gardens, or home-baked bread. Or they invited us over to their houses for Sunday dinner which, as a special treat, might include fried chicken. When I was six months old, we moved to Electra, Texas, where the same tradition prevailed.

But from the time I was two-and-a-half until almost six, my parents traveled around the MIdwest as Pentecostal evangelists, taking me with them, so the food situation changed. We usually stayed with the pastor's family wherever we went and ate with them or their church members, but when we were on the road, we ate in what my dad referred to as "greasy spoons." It might not have been high-class dining, but I loved every minute of it.

In 1944, Mom and I settled down in Waxahachie, Texas, so I could enter first grade. Mom taught piano at what was then Southwestern Bible Institute (SBI), a residential educational facility run by the Assemblies of God denomination which served students in the last two years of high school and the first couple of years of college. We lived in an apartment there while Dad continued to travel. I don't remember a thing about food in that apartment except that Mom grew a sweet potato in a glass of water, and the vine stretched all around the kitchen cabinets. When I entered second grade, Dad joined us as dean of men at SBI, and we moved to a little apartment in the boys' dormitory. If it had a kitchen, I don't remember it, either, because we always ate in the cafeteria, which was in the basement of the girls' dormitory.

That was fun. Mom liked it, too, because she wasn't that into cooking. In later years she liked to tell the story about how, on one of my birthdays as a child, I was complaining about not having a birthday cake, to which she responded, "Well, Pat, would you like me to bake you one?" After a moment's reflection, I answered sadly, "No, I guess not." Remembering that always made her laugh. To get back to the cafeteria, though, while we were waiting in line for our meals, we would sing choruses and silly songs along with the students, like this one to the tune of "Stars and Stripes Forever":

> *Be kind to your web-footed friend,*
> *For that duck may be somebody's mother.*
> *They live in a place called a swamp,*
> *Where it's always cold and damp.*
> *Now you may think that this is the end.*
> *Well, it is.*

That ending always tickled me because it was so unexpected, even when I knew what was coming. Second graders are easy to amuse.

Once in awhile, I would sleep in and Daddy would take me across the street to a tiny restaurant for breakfast. The memory that stays with me is how great it felt to have my daddy take me out to eat, just the two of us. On a few special occasions, our family drove the 30 miles to Dallas to have dinner with friends at Youngblood's. The fried chicken and biscuits with honey at this popular restaurant were so delicious that people would stand in a long line on the sidewalk to get a table. That was the most memorable dining experience of my early childhood and one that I wish I could repeat.

The summer before I entered third grade, my parents took a church in East St. Louis, Illinois, and we moved to Collinsville, about seven miles away. Dad planted a huge garden in the vacant lot next door, in which he grew some of the largest and tastiest produce I've ever seen. Our neighbors just up the street were farmers, and every time their cows got loose and ran down the road, Dad would hitch his little trailer to the car and take off after them to shovel up their manure for his garden. He grew just about everything edible, including green beans, which my parents put up every year in tin cans. I have never met anyone else who had a canner like ours, but it actually sealed the beans in cans just like the ones you get from the store. Of course we had no air-conditioning, so the canning process was hot in the summer, but it paid off in winter. Among other things, Dad grew rhubarb and gooseberries, from which Mom made pies (pie-baking was the one culinary art at which she was fairly skilled), but I never tasted them because I didn't like the way they looked. After I was grown and finally got up the nerve to taste them in pies, I realized what I had missed all those years.

We still were pretty poor in Collinsville, but Mom was an excellent money manager and she insisted that we eat out every Sunday. She maintained that since she was a co-pastor of the church and had to assist at both morning and evening services, she shouldn't have to cook dinner, too. ("Dinner," of course was eaten at noon. I was grown before I learned that more refined people reserved that term for the evening meal, which we called "supper.") Occasionally on Sundays, we ate at a little restaurant called the State Tavern in a brick building which had once been a service station on State Street in East St. Louis (now Martin Luther King Drive). It wasn't really a tavern, of course—our church didn't believe in drinking, so we never set foot in places that served drinks—but it had good cheeseburgers, of which I usually had two. Most Sundays, however, we ate at Pope's Cafeteria on Washington Street in downtown St. Louis, Missouri, which was just across the Mississippi from East St. Louis. With its excellent roast beef au jus and crispy fried chicken, Pope's was definitely a step up from our usual haunts. In fact, the recipe for one of Pope's desserts—a dense spice cake layered with bananas and meringue—was featured in the Sunday magazine of the *St. Louis Post-Dispatch.* I've often regretted that I didn't cut out that recipe and save it. My dad's sister, Wanda Faye, a gorgeous, fun-loving woman with enormous bosoms, was acquainted with the owner, Mr. Pope, through her work as a manicurist at the Missouri Athletic Club, and once when she was eating there with us, he came to our table to say hello.

There were several Pope's Cafeterias in St. Louis, but the one on Washington was the biggest, with seating on both the main floor and in the large basement. Even after I was married and had children, my husband and I sometimes accompanied my parents there, where we would meet the same people behind the counter who had served us when I was growing up. It was while she was sitting in a high chair in the basement of Pope's that our firstborn, Tamara, suddenly had a revelation: carefully picking up one pea at a time, she began flinging them around the room, smiling and exclaiming "Ball—whee!" When our three girls were a little older, we saw a stout young couple seated nearby with their two small, very chubby children. As children are inclined to do in cafeterias, these two had put more food on their trays than their stomachs could hold. While they sat there in tears, holding their forks over their plates, their parents kept yelling at them to "Eat it!" We felt sorry for the kids, but it was kind of funny, at the same time. When I returned to the St. Louis area to live in 1989, there were still one or two Pope's Cafeterias in the area, but the one on Washington was long gone, and the others closed down soon afterwards.

But I'm getting ahead of my story. In the mid-1950s, when MacDonald's was still advertising "Over 100,000 burgers sold!" and few married women had jobs outside the home, eating out was pretty rare for people in our income bracket—but not for our family. In addition to our regular Sunday dinners at Pope's, we ate once a week or so at little restaurants nearer to home. When I was a teenager, a scene occurred in one of them that I will always regret. Asking the waitress for some cornbread, a glass of milk, and a bowl, my dad proceeded to crumble the cornbread into the bowl, pour the milk over it, and eat the concoction with a spoon. I was so embarrassed that I left the table and sat in the car until the rest of the family had finished their meal. I'm sure no one in the restaurant paid any attention to Dad, and most parents would have dismissed my behavior as the amusing over-reaction of a teenager, newly obsessed with appearances. But, as I found out later, Dad was very upset that he had embarrassed me. I wasn't sensitive then to how painfully aware he was of the rough edges left by his poverty-stricken upbringing. It's one of those scenes in life that I would gladly do over if I had a chance.

While my social sensitivity was growing during those teen years, I was still unacquainted with finer dining until my junior year of high school, when a boy I was dating took me to a little restaurant called Le Petit Pigalle in the Windsor Hotel on Lindell Blvd. in St. Louis, which has since been torn down. It was there that I discovered filet mignon. Although I had been a voracious carnivore up to that time, my experience with beef had been limited to chuck roast or the occasional round steak. One taste of that tender, juicy, bacon-wrapped filet, and I was hooked. So after I married Harold Piety at the age of 19, I insisted that we go out for filet mignon every Tuesday at Augustine's, the best restaurant in Belleville, Illinois, where we were then living. Tuesday was Harold's payday, and, as I recall, one of those evenings would set us back around $8-$10. I know—that now sounds like a cheap meal for two at MacDonald's, but in 1958 Harold was bringing home only $80 a week as a sportswriter for the now-defunct *East St. Louis Journal*, so those dinners took a very significant bite out of our income.

Nine months and three weeks after we were married, I gave birth to our first daughter. In the meantime, my mother had invited us to move in with her and Dad and give them our rent money so she could put it in a savings account for us to accrue a downpayment on a house that my uncles would eventually build, with our help. Thanks to Mom's excellent money management, her brothers' carpentry skills, and a lack of zoning laws in their neighborhood, my parents' house was on a rather fancy, tree-lined street—Signal Hill Blvd.—even though their income was well below that of their neighbors. I remember Dad reporting with amazement around tax time after we first moved there in 1952 that he and Mom had earned $5,000 that year as pastors. The apartment in the basement had been built to host visiting evangelists who came to hold meetings at their church, but by the time I married, they had given up the church, which had been ravaged by internal politics, triggered by my elopement at age 14 with a member's son. Mom was teaching elementary school and Dad was operating a second-hand bookstore in East St. Louis and dealing in rare books through the mail. Aside from letting us live in their house, my parents didn't share any of their money with us, not only because they couldn't afford to, but because it was against their Depression-influenced philosophy. When kids grow up and get married, they should be responsible for themselves, they thought, and I agreed, which was why I insisted on paying them a small amount per month to cover utilities. Poor as Harold and I were, however, I refused to give up my dinners at Augustine's, which were even more important to me now that I spent most of my days in a one-room basement apartment, sleeping on a sofa bed, caring for an infant who slept in the same room, and watching soap operas on the black-and-white TV we had bought from Sears for $10 down and $10 a month.

I have a lot of things to be grateful to my mother for, but baby-sitting isn't one of them. While she generously allowed us to live under her roof—and we often went upstairs after dinner to play Scrabble with my parents—it was clear from the beginning that she did not intend to run a child care service. In fact, I never dared to ask her, except in emergencies. Still, I insisted on hiring a sitter so we could continue to go out to dinner on Tuesday evenings. Our most frequent sitters were Miss Alexander, an elderly "maiden lady" who lived on one side of my parents' house, and Lizzie, the African-American live-in maid and nanny for the Toberman family, on the other side. Thanks to Dad, I had grown up with a strong sympathy for American Blacks and an acute consciousness of the shameful treatment they were still receiving in our society, and I liked Lizzie very much, but

I'm embarrassed to realize now that, if I learned her last name, I never thought to dignify her existence by addressing her by it. That's another one of my big regrets, along with the one about Dad and the cornbread. Although it doesn't make up for my insensitivity about her name, we did, however, pay Lizzie the same rate as we paid Miss Alexander and wouldn't have considered doing otherwise.

Sometimes when I was ready for a dinner out, no sitters were available. Not to be deterred on such occasions, I would dispatch Harold to a rather nice Italian restaurant not far away to pick up our order of "two filet mignon dinners to go." Years later, when I laughingly recounted this episode in our married life to some more affluent friends (the husband was an attorney), Harold chided me after we got home for embarrassing him by revealing our "irresponsible financial behavior" as a young married couple. (Note to Harold: It was all my fault. Please accept my sincere apology more than half a century later.)

While I had enjoyed preparing dinner for my family when I was in high school (my mother paid me $20 a week to do so, since she wasn't fond of cooking and felt she had enough jobs already), I lost a lot of my enthusiasm for cooking after my marriage to Harold. For one thing, I had given birth to three daughters in three and a half years, which kept me very tired during the early years. For another, most of the time I was also either attending college, teaching school, or both, while being my own housekeeper. And, finally, cooking for someone who was so much better at it than I, and who couldn't resist pointing out my mistakes, took all of the fun out of it. So while our outings for filet mignon were seriously curtailed after the birth of our girls, I still argued for going out for a lot of our meals. Once when the girls were still young and I persuaded Harold to take us out to the Dog 'n Suds for dinner, I heard him mutter grumpily, "Next house we build isn't going to have a kitchen."

Harold liked to cook, and he was good at it. He also liked to grow food, and he especially loved roaming the countryside to pick wild blackberries. So we had some extraordinarily fine meals while the girls were growing up, with homemade bread and jams and fresh produce from our garden. He was an ace pie-baker, too, specializing in pecan, lemon meringue, and mincemeat, in addition to apple and cherry from the trees in our back yard when we lived in Dayton, Ohio. I loved everything Harold cooked, except the mincemeat pies, but I had a hard time containing my resentment when people congratulated me after our frequent dinner parties for having a husband who could cook. I was the one, after all, who had spent hours, and sometimes days, frantically cleaning the house, ironing the table cloth, arranging the table, and serving as *sous chef*. While I still was still the parent more often responsible for preparing the family's regular meals, Harold was the much-admired chef for all our dinner parties. Looking back, I realize that I was pretty lucky, as wives go, but I didn't always appreciate my good fortune then.

Eventually, Harold moved up in the newspaper world, becoming a member of the editorial board of the now-defunct *Dayton Journal Herald*, and I became a college English instructor, having worked my way through bachelor's and master's degrees while raising our three daughters. So although Harold and I never really got ahead financially, we were able to eat out fairly often (or maybe that was one reason why we never got ahead). One experience the whole family enjoyed was our weekly outings to Cassano's Pizza in Dayton. Their pizza still stands out in my memory as the best I have ever eaten. The crust was very thin and salty on the bottom, and the deluxe version that Harold and I liked was generously covered with ground sausage, pepperoni and finely diced onions, green peppers, and mushrooms, topped with mozzarella cheese. The slices were cut in squares, rather than triangles, and the toppings fairly weighted down the crust. Some 20 years later, on a motor trip with my mother to Hannibal, Missouri, I could hardly believe my eyes when I saw a billboard for Cassano's Pizza. I couldn't resist stopping in to give the place a try, and I discovered that the owners were related to the Cassano family in Dayton. But their pizza, which was OK, didn't seem as good as that we had enjoyed in Dayton.

Probably the highlight of our culinary experiences while I was married to Harold happened on a weekend in New York City. Harold had earned an extra $500 for a freelance editing job, and we decided to splurge on our first, and only, trip together to the Big City. Lutèce, an elegant French restaurant there, had been featured on the cover of the *New York Times Sunday Magazine*, and we were determined to give it a try. The first thing that made me realize that I had entered the upper stratosphere of dining is the fact that the menu the waiter gave me listed no prices; they were discreetly listed on Harold's menu, the implication being that women shouldn't bother their pretty little heads about money. We got off to a bad start, though, when Harold lit up a cigarette and ordered a cup of coffee before dinner. Such palate-killing working-class behavior obviously didn't go over with the waiter, who silently let his disapproval be known. I don't remember what Harold ordered, but I had a magnificent veal dish with fresh asparagus on the side and fresh strawberries with clotted cream for dessert. I will always remember Lutece, too, as the place where I developed a preference for unsalted butter; the sweet cream butter on their crusty French bread was the best I had ever tasted. We had no appetizer or salad, and, not being regular drinkers, we had ordered no drinks. Still, the bill for this repast, circa 1975, came to $49, plus tip—an awesome sum in our eyes. Throughout our meal, I had been surreptitiously eyeing a man dining alone near our table, trying to imagine the price he was paying, since he had drinks before, during, and after his rather generous meal. Harold and I were clearly out of our depth at Lutèce.

After Harold and I separated in 1977, though, I was rather quickly plunged into an orgy of fine dining when I went to work as editor for the Charles F. Kettering Foundation. One of the vice presidents there told me that when he had first joined the foundation staff, someone there told him, "You will never hear another word of criticism or eat a bad meal," because most people thought of foundations as places that gave away money. The Kettering foundation, however, is an "operating foundation," which means that it doesn't give away money; rather, it sponsors its own experimental projects, and in those days, at least, the staff didn't stint on lodging and meals when traveling on business, staying in hotels like the Capitol Hilton and Hyatt Regency in D.C. and the Algonquin in New York City, and dining in a host of fine restaurants, which were right up my alley.

Two of the most memorable culinary experiences of during my years with the foundation, though, took place in Ohio. Shortly after I joined the staff, I had the incredible good fortune of being asked to research and write the script for a documentary film about the life of Charles Kettering called "Boss Ket: One Man, Working With Others." Since Kettering had been a folksy sort of fellow, I had written the script with Jimmy Stewart in mind as host narrator. I even got all dolled up to go to the annual Air Force Hall of Fame dinner in Dayton, where I hoped to see Stewart and talk him into taking on the project, but, to my great disappointment, he didn't show up at the dinner and his people later turned down our request. Instead, we got E.G. Marshall, of "The Defenders" fame, who was getting on in years and had narrated a whole string of nature and historical documentaries. He was a good narrator, but he was no Jimmy Stewart, and the way he delivered some of my best lines was disappointing. Still, it was exciting to work with a man of his stature, so my colleague at the foundation, Emmet Frauman, who was coordinating work with the production company, screwed up his courage and asked our bosses if we could take Mr. Marshall out to dinner. "OK," they said, "but don't spend too much money."

We knew we were in trouble when Marshall said he had heard about a four-star restaurant in Cincinnati called "La Maisonette" that he would like to visit. And we began to sweat when he suggested that he would like to bring his make-up girl and several members of the production crew along. But how can you say no to E. G. Marshall? I have absolutely no idea what we ate that night. All I know is that Marshall ordered before-dinner drinks, wine with dinner, and after-dinner drinks for everyone, and the wait staff fell all over themselves to serve him, no doubt assuming—falsely—that he was paying the bill and would give them a large tip. I do remember the ride home in Emmet's car, in which he moaned all the way from Cincinnati to Dayton in anticipation of the hiding we were going to get from Jim Schwartzhoff, the foundation's crusty comptroller, for the humongous charge on Emmet's corporate American Express card. To our considerable relief, though, we got off without a scratch. I guess the foundation was as star-struck as we were and more than happy to have snagged the famous actor. The film was a hit, having a gala premier in the Old Court House in Dayton, and being aired on local public television in several cities, but I can't find it on the list of Marshall's films on the Web, so I guess it was very small potatoes to him.

My other unforgettable culinary experience in connection with the Kettering Foundation was the going-away champagne brunch the staff hosted for me when I left in 1982 to strike out for new horizons. My good friend and colleague, Mary Kay Abbas, and my secretary, the late, beloved Keta Kunke, organized and served it from the foundation kitchen, but the whole staff came, and there were toasts, poetic tributes, and even an illustrated lecture by the president, David Mathews, former secretary of HEW under President Ford. My good friend, the late Jim Kunde, head of the Urban Affairs division, who had given me my first contracts there, even presented me with a special award: a home-made trophy of a goofy bird made of feathers and styrofoam balls that had been originally created for someone who had accidentally set the former president's couch on fire. It had been traveling around to staff members who had managed to distinguish themselves in similar fashion, but the staff, Jim informed me, had decided to retire the trophy with me. (Don't ask.) That brunch, to which I wore a blond wig in an attempt to channel Marilyn Monroe, was one of the highlights of my life.

But the party wasn't over yet. When I joined the public affairs staff of the American Express Western Region Operations Center in Phoenix in1983, a whole new world of elegant dining opened up, including some memorable lunches in the famous Gold Room of the Arizona Biltmore. As speech writer for the senior vice president of the Western Region, I attended a number of well-catered management dinners at various Phoenix resorts like the Biltmore and the Pointe at Tapatio Cliffs, in addition to rather frequent parties the company threw for executives who were moving up or moving on. The company was an official sponsor of the Phoenix Open, as well as horse shows and, one year, the Senior PGA tourney. At these events I, along with my colleagues in Public Affairs, would staff the hospitality tents for important American Express clients. The food—sandwiches, vegetable trays, and drinks—was not especially distinguished, but the guests often were. I remember once, during a tent luncheon at a horse show, passing a bottle of wine to actor Lee Marvin, who politely declined. It was only then I remembered, with some embarrassment, having read that he had struggled with a drinking problem and was currently clean and sober.

There were more modestly priced places in Phoenix that I enjoyed eating in on my own time, too—the elegant little French Corner cafe at the corner of Camelback and Central, where my coworker Faye and I forged friendships with the musicians; Cafe Casino, a French cafeteria that served delicious French meals, including wine, for incredibly low prices; and Tokyo Express, a fast-food Japanese restaurant where I regularly enjoyed teriyaki chicken and sukiyaki beef bowls for a pittance. The French Corner and Cafe Casino are gone now, but whenever I'm in Phoenix, I always like to stop for a meal at Tokyo Express, which was still there last time I checked.

When I quit my job at American Express and returned to St. Louis in 1989 to be nearer to my aging parents, I went through a couple of very stressful years in which I wasn't sure the IRAs I had collected from the company were going to keep a roof over my head until I could find a job. The economy was still shaky from the Savings & Loan crisis, and I was 50 years old. Every job I applied for had 200 or more applicants. After a few months, I managed to piece together enough freelance writing and editing, along with part-time teaching for the community college, to squeak by, but by the time I found a steady job again, I had already cashed in my last IRA to pay the taxes on the ones I had been living on. Still true to form, however, I didn't stop eating out altogether.

I managed some rather nice lunches out with new friends, but more often I walked the half mile or so to Govinda's, the Hare Krishna restaurant on Lindell Blvd., which served pretty good vegetarian meals at very reasonable prices. I enjoyed smelling the incense and talking to Govinda and his Indian wife and little boy during these meals, and I even attended one of the services, out of curiosity. Govinda, I learned, had been born a Catholic but had never been able to understand why good things happen to bad people until he encountered the concept of reincarnation in the Hare Krishna movement, so he had converted and changed his name. But when I attended the service, I was struck by the similarities between it and the Catholic services I had attended—the incense, the chanting, and the "idols" were pretty much in the same in both, to me, who had grown up in an entirely different religious environment.

The full-time job that I eventually found in St. Louis was working for the president of a small college which by no means had the budget for the kinds of extravagant meals I had enjoyed at Kettering and American Express. Still, there were a few parties, like the annual alumni dinner dance at local hotels, and two or three times a year I attended large dinners at which a half dozen of the local big shots passed awards around to each other. The best thing about these dinners was dressing up in fancy evening wear and seeing people have fun, since the food was standard banquet fare—sometimes pretty good, but seldom anything to write home about.

In the days since my retirement, my dining out has been largely limited to fast food restaurants, with an occasional splurge at a nice sit-down establishment where the prices aren't too unreasonable. My old friend George and I go out to eat together once or twice a week, often at places reminiscent of the "greasy spoons" of my childhood, but a lot of times, I just have a sandwich or a bowl of cereal at home. It's OK, though—I've tasted life at its best and found it good.

Money

My mother was such a good money manager that, as a child, I never believed her when she said we were poor. We owned our own home (or, at least, we had a mortgage on it), we got a new car every year or two, and we ate out every Sunday (and sometimes during the week). That was back in the 1940s and '50s, when eating out was rare for the average family. We even had a library in our home, filled with hundreds of books. So how could we be poor?

Even when I was in high school, the truth hadn't yet hit me. "We earned $5,000 last year!" my dad proudly declared when he completed the family's 1952 income tax form. As a result of my mother's money management, her brother's carpentry skills, and the fact that there were no zoning laws in our unincorporated neighborhood, we were living in a rather affluent area back then, and as I walked down the tree-lined boulevard, looking at the large houses (a couple of which strongly resembled Tara, in "Gone With the Wind"), I thought, "I'll bet some people on this street made $10,000 last year."

I was more than startled when I discovered, a year or so later, that the father of one of my friends earned more than $10,000 a year by operating a crane that loaded barges on the Mississippi River. His was a family of high-school dropouts whose home looked like something out of "God's Little Acre," with junk cars in the yard and curtains separating the attic rooms. It was then I began to suspect that our neighbors had incomes of considerably more than $10,000 a year.

Mom was no Hetty Green, for sure, but we never lived like poor people, either, despite our relatively low income. "When I buy a car,

I put it on the longest terms I can," she told me, "and I make three payments every two months. That way, I can save interest by paying it off quickly, but if we have a hard month, I won't be behind in my payments and hurt my credit rating." She kept meticulous records of all her spending, giving ten percent of her income to the church, in addition to regular small sums to family members in need.

To really appreciate Mom's skills, though, you have to know that for several years our sole family income consisted of what our church members put in the offering plate—plus occasional gifts of homemade bread and home-canned food. My parents were Assemblies of God preachers, and their congregation seldom numbered more than 100 souls—all working class—so if the church hadn't stressed tithing—and if Mom hadn't been such a good money manager—we would have been out of luck.

By the time I graduated from junior high, Mom had earned her bachelor's degree from McKendree College in Lebanon, Illinois, and started teaching school in East St. Louis. After that, our family had a more dependable income stream, since the money Dad brought in was still mainly from the offering plate. As a preacher, he was never on salary that I know of. He said he thought he did better taking what people wanted to give. Although Dad couldn't match Mom's record-keeping ability, he had terrific survival skills, like all of the members of his family. Born dirt poor, the oldest of 10 living children of an uneducated itinerant Assemblies of God preacher, Dad had very few years of formal schooling (he was always vague about how many), and he had stumbled into preaching for a living when he was just 15 years old. By the time I was in grade school, his lifelong love of reading had led to a sideline of collecting and trading in rare books, which, in turn, led to his learning to hand-tint antique prints with transparent water colors. He taught himself to mat these prints, which he found in old county atlases, and, eventually, he bought some framing tools and learned how to frame them. But even before he took up framing, he had figured out how to track down the descendants of people who had lived in the fine homes pictured in these tomes and talk them into buying the prints for $30 or $40 apiece. Since he usually paid only $5 for an atlas, which could contain many prints, his profit margin was fairly large.

Mom, overlooking the time, skill and effort Dad had put into finding and preparing the prints and the people whose ancestors had lived in the homes, often accused him of overpricing this art. She didn't really understand the capitalist principle of market forces—which is ironic, since Dad was the philosophical communist of the family. What Mom understood from her German, working-class parents was to work hard and make every penny count. While Dad was no stranger to hard work, whether it was visiting the sick, tending to his magnificent produce garden, or performing maintenance jobs around our property, he had a more entrepreneurial spirit and a bit of the "lilies of the field" philosophy acquired from the Sermon on the Mount.

Despite their ability to make a little money go a long way—or perhaps because of it—both my parents were risk-takers, and neither ever had a day of experience in the corporate, workaday world. So, put in perspective, my personal history with respect to money shouldn't be totally surprising. It is still rather shocking, though, even to me.

I think I inherited a bit—if only a bit—of money management skills from my mother. At least on occasion I have been rather clever in making a dollar go a long way. I like to tell people how I managed to send my youngest daughter to college for more than two years on a $1,000 certificate of deposit. It isn't entirely true, but it makes a good story. When her father and I divorced, we pocketed about $5,000 apiece, the sum total of our savings and profits accumulated during 20 years of marriage. Since one of our daughters was already in college and the other two were heading there fast, I suggested to him, "You've always earned twice as much as I have, so why don't you send two daughters to college, and I'll send one?" and he agreed. Don't ask me what happened to the $5,000 I got out of the divorce. I guess most of it went toward the expenses of moving into and furnishing my new apartment, since I took nothing with me but my clothes, a table, a TV, a record player, some plants and several pictures. In any case, by the time Julia was ready for college, I had only $1,000 left in a CD. Luckily, she chose to go to Oklahoma State University, one of the least expensive state schools in the nation. OSU tuition was just under $1,000 a semester in 1981, so I took out a loan from the credit union to pay for her first semester, using my CD as security. I paid her room and board—plus monthly installments on the loan—out of my regular paychecks. She started to college in January, and by the beginning of the fall semester I had paid off the first loan and was ready to take out another one. I repeated this process for the next two years, until she married a graduate student in her junior year.

At that point, having over-absorbed the lesson from my mother that, once your children are married or graduate from college, they should be self-supporting, I discontinued my support for Julia's education, except for an occasional small loan. To Julia's credit, she managed to graduate, and, with help from a supportive husband and the federal student loan program she went on to law school after her second marriage, graduating number one in her class, and is now a successful partner in a law firm in Oklahoma. Although I had always thought she would be an actress or singer, I should have suspected she would end up in law when, still an undergraduate, she got a divorce from her first husband for less than $100 by following the instructions in a book on how to write your own divorce that she found in the college library.

Many years later, my eldest daughter, Tamara, got accepted into Harvard Law School to pursue her LLM. Still suffering from guilt over not helping my children more financially while they were in college, I was determined to be more supportive this time. But while I had a good job with a decent salary, I was in the same financial shape I had always been, which is to say I had no savings and was living from paycheck to paycheck. So I took in a boarder. For each of the nine months while she was working on her LLM, the grandson of a friend in Pennsylvania lived in the guest room in my condo and wrote out a check to my daughter for his rent. It wasn't a lot of money for a law student at Harvard, but I was proud of having figured out a way to at least contribute to my daughter's higher education. (Tamara R. Piety is now a tenured law professor and the author of *Brandishing the First Amendment*, MIchigan University Press, 2012.)

In case you're wondering why I never accumulated any money, the answer is simple: I spent every penny I could spare on traveling and eating out. Not only did I fail to save money, but I actually mortgaged my future: In the course of my long and varied career, I quit several jobs rather precipitously, and more than once I cashed in the retirement funds I had accumulated in order to finance a trip. The first time was after I stopped teaching third grade to go back to school full-time and get my bachelor's degree (in those days, you could teach school on a provisional certificate in Illinois while working on a degree). I used that retirement fund to finance a family road trip to my husband's father's home in San Francisco. The next really big trip paid for with retirement funds came after I suddenly, and with a characteristically dramatic flourish, resigned from my position as an English instructor at Wright State University in Ohio when the department decided to switch from using instructors to graduate assistants (a popular modern practice among universities which, I believe, demonstrates the institutions' emphasis on acquiring students as opposed to providing them with a high-quality education). This time, I gave my eldest daughter a trip to Europe as a high school graduation present—with me tagging along. Neither of us had ever been abroad, but, using Arthur Frommer's guidebooks, we traveled to London, Paris, and Nice, staying in B&Bs, riding trains, taking the ferry one way across the English Channel and a hydroplane coming back. It was the trip of a lifetime, and I'll never regret it, even if I end up living on the street, which my friend George reminds me is still a possibility.

Of course I knew when I took Tamara to Europe that I would have to do the same for the other two girls when they graduated. Titi (short for "Tiger") was due to graduate in two years and Julia in four, and I had no idea where I would get the money. But somehow I did. I recall an unexpected $900 refund from the IRS which the girls' dad generously donated to the cause, and I must have saved some money and/or taken out a loan or two, but, one way or another, I came up with the cash. Actually, Titi wasn't sure she wanted to go abroad with me, and she suggested that maybe she would prefer to have a car, instead. When I recovered somewhat from my hurt feelings, I told her that since I had planned to go with her, I would give her half of the money our trip would have cost, and she decided to opt for the trip. She didn't want to go anywhere that English wasn't the national language, so we limited our travels to London, Bath, and Edinburgh. This is especially ironic in retrospect, since a few years later she won a Fulbright Fellowship to Denmark, where she lived for eight years, becoming fluent enough in Danish to translate two works by Danish philosopher Soren Kierkegaard (*Repetition and Philosophical Crumbs*, Oxford World's Classics, 2009). Somewhere along the way, she also acquired proficiency in German and several other languages. Julia, our third daughter, wanted to visit as many countries as possible, taking only a shoulder bag apiece, so that's what we did, traveling on a Eurailpass to several cities in Germany, Austria, Italy, and France. One of the many highlights of that trip was having a couple of muscle-bound beach boys try to pick us up on the beach at the Lido. (Oh, to be in my 40s again!)

In between the trips with daughter number two and daughter number three, I visited my mother in Asuncion, Paraguay. I have no memory of how I paid for that trip, either, but I was determined to keep my promise to her. And, besides, how could anyone resist a trip to somewhere so exotic as Paraguay? Not my mother, certainly. At the age of almost 67, she had decided to sell her car, rent out her house, and go off to Paraguay to teach math and music in Asuncion Academy, an interdenominational, English-language grade school/high school. She didn't know anyone in there, nor did she have more than a rudimentary knowledge of Spanish, and the country was still under the control of the notorious dictator, Alberto Stroessner, but when she said she was thinking of going, I promised her that if she did, I would come down to visit her. We had a great time, taking day trips by car with her colleagues and new-found friends to places like the famous Iguazu Falls, on the border with Brazil and Uruguay.

On my way home, I even flew Mom with me to Rio de Janeiro, where we stayed for a couple of nights in the swanky Intercontinental Hotel on the beach and fantasized about being jet-setters. Late on the second night, as we were sitting in the coffee shop, Mom noticed a rather plain, 30-something woman sitting by herself. "See that woman?" she said. "I like to fantasize about people. I'll bet she's a school teacher who has saved up her money to come down here to look for a husband."

"Well, Mom," I said, "If you weren't my mother and you saw me here, what would you think about me?"

"Oh, I don't think I should say," she demurred.

I couldn't let that pass, so I pressed her further.

"I would think you were an adventuress," she finally said, with a shy smile. Her use of such an old-fashioned word amused me, and it also suggested to me that I had long played the role of surrogate for my mother's fantasies. If anyone was an adventuress at heart, I suspect it was Mom, but as far as I know, she did her best to walk the straight and narrow as a lady preacher, even after my parents's 34-year marriage ended in divorce and Dad eventually married again.

While we were in Rio, a Palestinian businessman whom I had never met took us out to dinner. His brothers had become friends with my former husband and me while my husband was writing editorials on the MIddle East for a Dayton, Ohio, newspaper, and when they heard I was going to Rio, they urged me to look up their youngest brother, who owned a clothing factory there. So I called him and he took us to dinner one evening at a restaurant high up in the shell of an unfinished building, from the terrace of which we could look across the bay at the famous Christ of the Andes statue. As we were admiring this marvel, he graciously offered to drive us up the mountainside to see it after dinner. I will never forget this act of generosity from our Palestinian friends. Later, Mom confessed to me that when I had first told her a Palestinian man I had never met was going to take us to dinner in Rio, she had some doubts, but, as I have already explained, I come from a family of risk-takers.

My rather extensive traveling is a major reason I never accumulated any wealth, so I actually spent my last couple of working years scoping out potential places around St. Louis to sleep and take showers in the event that I ended up homeless after my retirement. I had things worked out fairly well in my imagination, although I could never figure out how to get nutritious meals without a kitchen. "You seem to think that having money is sinful," my daughter Tamara said to me once, and I suspect there's more than a grain of truth in that. I know I appear to have gone out of my way sometimes to avoid accumulating any wealth.

As a token minority on the president's cabinet at a small college in St. Louis, I made approximately half the salary of most of my fellow cabinet members. At one point, the president, in what may have been a rare fit of guilt for underpaying me, gave me a contract for $10,00 extra a year to "help him with his mail." When it became obvious that he was willing to accept little or no help with his mail, I bugged him so much about not getting enough work to justify my extra pay that he cancelled the contract at the end of the first quarter. My failure to fight for bigger salaries was no doubt a result of my dad's socialist tendencies, his empathy for the poor, and the emphasis he put on the teachings of Jesus in the New Testament about its being easier for a camel to go through the eye of a needle than for a rich man to enter into heaven, etc. Not that I have any expectations of heaven—I just shy away from the idea of having more money than I need when so much of the world is so poor.

As my friend George points out, though, I am remarkably inconsistent on the subject of money. While I have never spent much on anything beside travel and eating out (I buy virtually all of my clothes on sale or in thrift stores and spend next to nothing on cosmetics and hair care), I do enjoy a lot of the things that money can buy. Among my friends are a few moderately wealthy people, and I enjoy visiting in their homes and being treated to the occasional dinner in a nice restaurant. Since several of my jobs were in public affairs, I often got to attend functions at fancy resorts, stay in nice hotels, and eat in classy restaurants on my employers' tab, something I never complained about. I was even in love with a rich playboy for more years than I care to admit, and I relished riding in his Jaguar, Corvette, and Bentley. I never made it to Rolls Royce status in his little black book, but skinny-dipping at midnight in his pool is an experience I won't soon forget.

Still, I prefer for wealth to remain, largely, in other people's hands, where I feel less guilty about it. I do like the idea of grand public buildings that everyone can enjoy, like museums and libraries and those wedding palaces from Soviet Union days, as opposed to the obscenely palatial private homes of business moguls I see pictured on the Internet and in magazines featuring the rich and famous. Besides, I don't want the responsibility of taking care of all that stuff, paying the taxes on it, worrying about losing it, or carrying around the guilt that I know would be mine. I'm content to feast occasionally on the crumbs that fall from the rich folks' tables.

Some smart lady—I can't remember who—said, "I've been rich and I've been poor, and rich is better," and I have to concede that she probably knew whereof she spoke. At least once in my adult life I was precariously close to poverty, and it was no fun, believe me. In 1989, when I quit my job with American Express in Phoenix to move to St. Louis, near my aging and ailing parents, I thought I would have no problem finding another position, but I was dead wrong. Although I had a good resume, the St. Louis job market was suffering aftershocks from the 1987 stock market plunge. Every job I applied for had at least 200 applicants, and no one seemed interested in hiring a 50-year-old woman who claimed to have quit a good job in the middle of a recession. (American Express policy forbade its human resources department to provide any information on a former employee beyond job title and dates of employment, so I had no way of proving that I had not been fired.) To make a miserably long story short, I will simply say that I spent the last IRA paying the taxes on the others that I had cashed in to live on, supplemented by a small, sporadic income from freelance editing and teaching English at the community college part-time. During that time, I had what I call a "walking nervous breakdown." Since I had no health insurance, I couldn't afford to go to a counselor, so I just had to muddle through.

One would think that such an experience would cure me of ever doing anything so reckless again, but one would be wrong. When I was

58 years old, I left my job at the aforementioned college to become managing editor of *Review,* the economics journal of the Federal Reserve Bank of St. Louis. That was the kind of job no sane person would ever leave voluntarily, considering the benefits program. But after almost losing my eyesight trying to correct all the subscripts and superscripts that got turned into alphabet soup every time a Ph.D. economist emailed a PC-generated article down to the Apple-using graphic artists for layout, I completely lost it one day when someone discovered a typo on the cover. Among the list of articles inside, the word "debt" had somehow come out as "debit." It wasn't the first error that had slipped by me, and I was mortified beyond the bounds of sanity. Without another word, I went to my computer and composed an email to my boss, informing him that I was giving two weeks' notice and would be working from home for the duration of my employment.

That was a Friday morning. For the rest of the weekend, I lay around on my couch moaning, "What have I done? What have I done?" I was a few months shy of 60 years old. I had a mortgage and a car note coming due every month, not to mention expenses like food and health care, but I had no savings and approximately $300 in my checking account.

As it turned out, what could have been a genuine tragedy had a happy ending. The president of the college took me back the following Monday, so that I ended up being paid by both employers over the next two weeks. I like to think that I was rehired because of my writing and editing skills, and not because I had been involved for several years in a clandestine affair with the (unmarried) chairman of the board (the aforementioned rich playboy), but I guess the publications I produced for that institution thereafter will have to serve as evidence for or against my case.

So at the age of almost 60, I had to start all over accumulating funds for my retirement. When I retired, five years later, I sold my condo to a friend for a good profit (although not nearly as good as it could have been if I had bothered to check out the market). With the profits, I was able to pay off my credit cards and car note and make a down payment on a darling little 100-year-old house on a large, wooded lot in Stillwater, Oklahoma, an hours' drive away from two of my daughters. Gazing at the roses on the picket fence and the crape myrtles and magnolias as I gently rocked in the porch swing that stretched along the whole east side of my little house, I continually had to pinch myself to be sure that I wasn't dreaming.

To supplement my income, I taught English at Oklahoma State University, where one of my first classes met in the very same room that

I had sat in for freshman composition almost half a century before. Later, I also taught at Northern Oklahoma College, and, after that, I served as a columnist and reporter for the *Stillwater NewsPress*. Writing the column was my favorite job of all times, and it made me a whole raft of wonderful friends, even though it paid the grand sum of $10 per column. So I can personally testify that money isn't everything when it comes to job satisfaction. Eventually, though, I realized that I wouldn't have either enough money or energy to maintain my house and yard in Stillwater much longer, so I succumbed to the siren lure of the city, selling my beloved little house and returning to St. Louis.

Somehow, though, I have managed to take a number of great trips since my retirement, including one to Argentina and one to attend President Obama's first inauguration, where I stood out on the Mall in the freezing cold all day beside a young friend in her 20s who had helped me drive from St. Louis to D.C. Last summer, I took a delightful trip to the south of France, staying for a few days with an ex-sister-in-law on her organic farm outside Aix-en-Provence and spending a few more days in a fabulous old hotel in Vieux Lyon with my daughter Tamara.

Now that my 75th birthday is only a few weeks away and my laughably small savings are getting smaller all the time (they would finance maybe two more trips like the last one to France), my friend George keeps reminding me that I could still end up as a bag lady if I don't change my ways. I can only respond with an anecdote that my mother used to tell about her brother Jim, a hyperactive, multi-talented, athletic risk-taker. When he was growing up, she said, people were always telling him that he was going to kill himself someday with the stunts he pulled. To which he would always reply with an impish grin, "Haven't yet!" He lived to his mid-80s. I should be so lucky.

Bicycles

I'm having a hard time resisting the urge to start this essay by telling you how I stole my bicycle back from a bicycle thief, but that didn't happen until I was in my 30s, and I like to tell these stories in chronological order, so you'll have to wait. And, anyway, it wasn't, technically, my bicycle.

My first and only bicycle while I was growing up must have arrived when I was about eight years old, because by the time my little brother was a toddler, I was riding him all around the neighborhood in the basket, and he was born less than three months before I turned nine. It was a red bike, and Daddy bought it for me for Christmas. I say Daddy because I'm not sure Mom would have bought it if it had been up to her. She was always saying how poor we were, although I could never tell it, and the bike must have taken a huge bite out of their very limited income from the offering plate on Sundays. Mom never had a bicycle of her own when she was growing up, being reduced to riding her younger brother's whenever he wasn't using it—and also having to ride it in a skirt, since Grandpa didn't allow his girls to wear pants. So, maybe, left to her own devices, Mom wouldn't have bought me a bike. But Daddy liked to give his little girl everything he reasonably could, like the baton he bought me when I was in fifth grade and all the girls were dreaming of becoming majorettes, or the shoe skates I got in junior high, which indirectly got me into a lot of trouble because roller-skating was how I got involved with the boy I unsuccessfully ran away to marry at 14.

But I digress.

I will never forget the day I got that first bike. We had already opened our other presents, and I was probably kind of disappointed at having gotten nothing very great, when Daddy insisted that we go visit some people from our church, right now! It seemed like a strange thing to do on Christmas day, but all was revealed when we got to Brother and Sister Hodge's house and Daddy brought this shiny new bicycle up out of their basement. I can tell you that had to be the most exciting Christmas of my childhood, even better than the one when I sneaked downstairs in the middle of the night and spotted a blonde bride doll standing under the tree, and a whole lot better than the Christmas when my parents gave me a ping-pong net, balls, and paddles, but no table.

Anyway, I loved that bike. I don't remember how we got it home from the Hodges' house or who taught me to ride it (although my money is on Daddy there, too), but I can tell you that very soon I was riding that bike everywhere, a mile to school and up and down the hills on the black-topped roads in our edge-of-town neighborhood. I remember riding for blocks and blocks with no hands—and certainly no helmet—although I always held onto the handles when my baby brother was in the basket, and we never had an accident. I am still amazed at how casual my parents were about their children's safety when I look back on those times! I would never have let one of my children ride my toddler in the basket of her bike or, for that matter, drive a car around the neighborhood with several kids in it when she was no more than 12 years old, which, if you have read the essay on cars, you already know that I did. Times were definitely different back then.

For about four years, that bike was a central part of my childhood, until one day I decided to take it apart to paint it. I never got around to painting it, and I know I couldn't find all the parts to put it back together, so that was the end of the bike-riding days of my youth, since I never got another bike. As I recall, my little brother had at least two when he was growing up, but I'm not counting. Really.

I do have one other significant memory about that bike, though. We lived on a corner, where Carl Street made a sharp right turn and went up the hill to the Waggoners' farm, passing, on its way, the Golightlys', my Uncle Jim's, the Schmidts' and the Deans' houses on one side and the Matikitises', the Wendlers' and the Rapps' on the other. When I was about eleven, Uncle Jim and Aunt Elsie sold their brick house to a family with a teen-aged daughter. It was the nicest house on the block, having been built by my Uncle Jim, who was one heck of a carpenter, and the people who bought it seemed a little out of place in our working class, semi-rural neighborhood. I heard that the father owned a paper box company, although probably he was only a manager in a paper box company, but they seemed to put on airs, and they had a station wagon with wood trim and the box company logo, as well as a convertible which their only child, the teen-aged daughter, drove around town with the top down.

When they first moved in, the new lady of the house gave my mother and me a tour, and she didn't seem to flinch when she opened her daughter's closet door and there was a box of Kotex up on the shelf. That just about blew me away, because I had recently started my periods, and even though Dad had told me where babies came from when I was only five years old, I was too embarrassed to tell my mother that I had started menstruating, so she had to find out by accident. It was really hard for me to talk to my mother about personal things; on the few occasions when I made a stab at it, I always felt a lump in my throat. I think I was afraid she might use the information to hurt me later on. But, of course, it was inevitable that she would find out, and once she did, she gave me a little lecture about how a girl could do anything during her period that she did the rest of the time, including riding horses and taking baths, which some girls didn't do back then. And she didn't try to hide her contempt for girls who took on about their cramps or thought they should be exempted from certain chores during those times. That was the only time we talked about it, and I never got over being embarrassed about the whole subject, so I was fascinated by how cool the neighbor lady was when she opened her daughter's closet door and there was a box of Kotex, right up on the shelf where anyone could see it. She acted as if it were the most normal thing in the world.

Maybe her mom's casual air—plus the convertible—is why the new neighbor girl came to symbolize the epitome of sophistication in my mind at the time. I desperately wanted to make friends with her, but she was several years older than I and didn't even know I existed. So by now you're probably wondering how a bicycle figures in all this. Well, one of the things I liked to do was ride my bike up Carl Street to the Waggoners' farm and coast back down the hill, often with no hands, so, for the better part of one afternoon following our tour of the new neighbor's house, I rode my bike up the incline toward the Waggoners' farm and slowly coasted back down again, trying hard to work up the nerve to turn into the new neighbors' driveway, go up to the door, ring the bell, and introduce myself to that girl. But I never did, and we moved to Belleville the summer after I graduated from eighth grade, so the dreamed-of friendship never materialized.

Fast forward a bunch of years, through the incredibly sweet times when Harold and I bought our oldest daughter, Tamara, her first bike at the hardware store in O'Fallon, Illinois, and took turns teaching her to ride it, through the successive bicycles and riding lessons for the other girls, to the early 1970s, when we were living in our beloved house in the Dayton View neighborhood of Dayton, Ohio. One of my most vivid bicycle memories from that time was when our middle daughter, Titi, appeared at the front door, followed closely by an angry stranger, and threw herself into my arms, in tears. Titi had been trying out her sister Julia's new three-speed bicycle when, unfamiliar with handbrakes, she had accidentally run in front of a car, which had almost hit her. The man at the door was the visibly shaken driver, who told me in no uncertain terms that I should not allow my children to ride on the streets with cars when they didn't know how to handle a bike. He was right, of course, but what I remember most is holding Titi in my arms, because running to me in tears was totally not her style. Since birth, she has always been an extremely self-sufficient person, and that is the only time I remember her coming to me for solace since she was a toddler and suffering from an undiagnosed illness, so I was very touched by it.

And now, on a lighter note, we come to the part I hinted at in the beginning: Although there was a more-than-average amount of crime in our Dayton View neighborhood in the 1970s, Julia and I always left our bikes unlocked and parked on the front porch at night. We figured that since they weren't the fancy kind of bicycles thieves usually coveted, and since the porch was right outside the dining room, no one would bother to try to steal them. Wrong.

One night, probably when Harold and I were engaged in our fierce battle for ping-pong superiority in the basement, we heard our dog, Jill, barking furiously upstairs, but we didn't bother to check on her, since Jill was a Nervous Nelly, and lots of things could move her to a frenzy of barking. Besides, I was so set on trying to win even one game against Harold that probably a tornado wouldn't have torn me away from the table. In any case, when we got up the next morning and went out on the porch, the bikes were gone. If you've ever had anything stolen from you, you can imagine how violated we felt—not to mention that we now had no bikes to ride and certainly not enough money to replace them.

So, a few weeks later, when I drove past a house in Lower Dayton View (an area with more poverty and crime than Upper Dayton View, where we lived) and saw Julia's stolen bike parked on the sidewalk in front of a house, my sense of injustice, not to mention my desire for vengeance, went into high gear. Parking the car at the curb, I went up to the house and knocked on the door. "Do you know who this bike belongs to?" I asked the young woman who opened the door. "Yes," she answered, "it belongs to our friend, Ike." "No it doesn't; it belongs to me," I exclaimed with righteous indignation, "somebody stole it from our house!" Technically speaking, it belonged to Julia, but I figured that, as the adult parents, Harold and I had the right to claim ownership of all family property.

At that point, the girl stepped out on the porch, closed the front door and lowered her voice. "We think he stole something from us, too. He's inside and we have called the police." In retrospect, her story sounds pretty fishy. What a coincidence that her family would have called the police about a theft at the very moment I happened to pass by and see Julia's bicycle out front! But the thought occurred to me, at the time, that I wouldn't be able to provide proof of ownership to the police, since we had never registered it or had Julia's name engraved on it, and I had no idea where the sales receipt was. Someone had removed the fenders, but I was certain it was Julia's missing bike; it was a yellow, three-speed J.C. Penney model that I had never seen the likes of around our neighborhood, or anywhere else, for that matter.

So I jumped on it and headed toward home, racing past the stately Grace Methodist Church and up the bumpy brick street of Amherst Place to number 1230, our home, pedaling as fast as my 36-year-old legs could go. Realizing that the thief could drive by the house and see the bicycle if I put it back on the porch, I stowed it in the garage next to, and slightly behind, the house.

But then there was the problem of our family station wagon, which I had left parked in front of the house where I had found the bicycle. All I could do was walk the four or five blocks back down the hill to my car, hoping all the way that I would not encounter the erstwhile and now, no doubt, angry bicycle thief. Just as I was turning on the engine and getting ready to back out of my parking place, a tall guy (in my mind, he is wearing a big hat, but that may be my overly vivid imagination) came out of the house where I had talked to the girl.

"Hey!" he yelled.

Acting as if I didn't hear him, I continued slowly backing up.

"Hey!" he yelled again. "Did you take a bike from in front of this house!"

Rolling down the window and giving him my best wide-eyed, dumb-blonde look (even though I am a brunette), I replied, "I don't know what you're talking about" and drove off. It wasn't the first lie I had ever told—lying does not come naturally to me, so I tend to do it only when lives are in danger—but I figured this was one of those times, and the life in danger was mine.

We never recovered the other bike, and for the next few weeks, I was a little anxious about whether the thief would come back and take revenge, but that never happened, either. I have to admit, though, that stealing back Julia's bike was one of the high points of my life. I felt like Robin Hood. I even considered, in passing, a career as one of those people who recover children from the non-custodial parents who have kidnapped them. But, as I have done with several other situations in my life—like the first and only time I tried inline skating at the age of 60 and didn't fall down—I decided to quit while I was ahead. The nagging thought does occur to me, on occasion, that maybe it wasn't really Julia's bike, although I was certain it was, at the time—and still am. Pretty much.

I guess the rest of this essay will be anticlimax after that story, but I do feel obliged to mention the happy days with my second husband when we would ride our bikes together along the bike path running for more than 20 miles beside the Miami River in Dayton. My first husband, Harold, had never shown any interest in some of the things I had liked to do when I met him, such as roller-skating, swimming and riding bikes. He much preferred working in his garden, reading, or listening to Beethoven, so it was really a delight to have a partner who liked to have fun with me. Evan, the aforementioned second husband, was also a marathon runner, so I often rode my bike alongside him as he took his 6-to-10-mile daily run through the neighborhood. Those companionable bike rides, as well as several road trips we took across the U.S. and through much of Mexico, are among my best memories of that short-lived relationship.

After my divorce from Evan, while I was living in Phoenix, I kept my bicycle, but I didn't have much time to ride it because my job at American Express was so time-consuming and stressful. So stressful, in fact, that I developed a heart irregularity. When the doctor discovered it, I told him it was probably caused by stress, but he insisted on putting me on a heart regulator (Quinaglute) that gave me intense chest pain and made me unable to exert much physical energy, so that I ended up flunking all the stress tests at the Arizona Heart Institute and had to have my heart catheterized. After that ordeal, the doctors at the Heart Institute said to me, "Your arteries look great. They must constrict when you are under stress." Right.

Convinced that my original self-diagnosis had been correct, I rejected the nitroglycerin my doctor wanted to give me for the chest pains that I hadn't had until he prescribed the Quinaglute and, against his advice and that of my friends, I slowly weaned myself off the Quinaglute, telling myself that if I died of a heart attack, there were worse ways to go. I eventually got back into shape enough to climb Squaw Peak and participate in other reasonably vigorous physical activities. Later, when I went to a different doctor—a cardiologist unaffiliated with my earlier doctor or the Arizona Heart Institute— and told him what I had done, he said I never should have been put through all that the trauma and risk to my health in the first place. It was a waste of my money and that of the insurance company, he said.

Shortly after that, though, someone stole my bicycle and I didn't try to get it back, so I had to content myself with working out at the nearby community college gym, hiking up Central Avenue past Sen. John McCain's house once a week with my friend Judy Contreras, and swimming in one of the four pools at the apartment complex where I lived. (In winter, I liked to put my beach towel in the oven before going out to the pool at night, so I could wrap myself in a warm towel upon finishing my solitary moonlight swim.)

Aside from the exercise bike I rode with feverish determination when I fell in love with the Olympic athlete in Phoenix, I didn't get another bicycle until well after I was 50 years old, a few years after I moved to St. Louis. It was a sparkly white 7-speed bike with concealed gears, an old-fashioned seat, and old-fashioned foot brakes, but I'm afraid of riding on city streets, so I had to load it up on my bike rack and take it to Tower Grove Park, where I could ride on the relatively level paths in that lovely old Victorian garden. But since that was a lot of trouble, and since I didn't have anyone to ride with, I didn't do it much.

When I moved to Stillwater, Oklahoma, after my retirement, I took the bike with me and rode it a bit, but I was still afraid of riding on the street and I didn't know of any handy bike trails, so I didn't ride it much there, either. Somewhere during that time, my youngest daughter, Julia, bought herself a bike so we could take rides together, but we only did it a couple of times because she was very busy, and she lived more than an hour's drive away, and I had trouble with my bike rack. I was touched by her gesture, though.

The bike I had then—the sparkly white one I had bought in St. Louis—was a nice one, and still is, as anyone can see who comes to visit me, as it is currently sitting in the bedroom of my apartment in St. Louis, having traveled through several residences I have called home and having been virtually unridden for years. From time to time, I pay $60 or so to have it tuned up, and a few years ago, I bought some new tires for it. A couple of years ago, I bought a lovely, large seat that looks as if it would really be comfortable to ride.

Does anybody want to buy a sparkling white retro bicycle that has only been ridden by a little old lady on weekends?

Death

It could be fairly said that the most enduring relationship of my life has been my relationship with death. Being the daughter of two ministers, I periodically found myself waiting around in funeral parlors with my parents as the friends and relatives of a church member came to pay their last respects to a loved one, or sitting through services for people I barely knew as my mom provided the music and my dad delivered the eulogy. In one of my early memories, I am standing with a playmate from church beside the coffin of someone I have long since forgotten while we take turns scaring each other with the notion that we saw the dead person's hand move.

When I wasn't hanging out at the funerals of church members or their families, I could often be found at the funerals of my mom's relatives in Southern Illinois. Grandma Rainbolt, born when her mother was 46 years old, was the youngest of 13 children. My mother didn't have me until she was 27, so by the time I was old enough to notice, many members of Grandma's large family were already beginning to die off. When one of them did, everyone—grandparents, aunts, uncles, cousins, great-aunts, great-uncles, and second and third cousins—gathered at the graveside to re-establish ties and catch up on the news. And just to be sure that no one in Mom's large clan was ever forgotten, she and her two sisters—often accompanied by me and sometimes my brother—made annual "30th of May" or "Decoration Day" trips to Marion, Illinois, to place flowers on their graves.

Now that I think about it, I'm amazed to realize, however, that I don't recall attending a single funeral for a member of my Dad's family.

Although it was also very large (he was the eldest of 10 living children and his mother was one of 13), the Chamless family was less clannish and more spread out geographically, and, from what Grandma Chamless told me about her childhood, I gather that several of her siblings died young from accidents in those Wild West days in Texas and Oklahoma. So I suspect those who survived were more focused on living life to the fullest than remembering the dead.

Nevertheless, death was a dominant, if not particularly grisly, presence in my childhood. But familiarity with a phenomenon is not the same as understanding it. Although I knew rationally that someday I would die, that event seemed so far in the future as to be inconceivable, and the idea that life could exist without me was beyond my comprehension. What filled me with dread, though, was the knowledge that, in all probability, my parents would die before me. Perhaps in an effort to steel myself against this unthinkable catastrophe, I periodically engaged in dramatic fantasies about how I would feel when they were gone forever. Far from strengthening my defenses, however, this exercise in personal theater never failed to fill me with horror and always ended with me wracked by sobs.

Growing up in a Pentecostal environment, I heard a fair number of hellfire-and-brimstone sermons (although not from my dad, thank goodness), in which the dying sinner felt the flames of hell lapping up around his bed as he sank begging for mercy toward his horrendous fate. Those sermons were enough to bring many an adult sobbing to the altar, not to mention scarring an innocent child for life, but as far as I can tell, my fear of hellfire has long since receded deep into my subconscious, if not into oblivion. It's the idea of *not living*—rather than the fear of going to hell—that I have always struggled with.

When I was teaching freshman English at Wright State University in Dayton, Ohio, in the 1970s, one of my students startled me by asking if I had an obsession with death, since I had assigned so many stories and poems about it. In my defense, I pointed out that the readings had all been taken from the textbook, which had been chosen by a department committee. But he did make me think. A significant number of what we consider the great writers seem to be preoccupied with death, and Tolstoi's masterpiece, "The Death of Ivan Ilyich," was eerily accurate in predicting the stages of death and dying that, 100 years later, Dr. Elizabeth Kubler-Ross would outline in her famous work.

So an obsession with death may not be all that abnormal. I was horrified to learn from some of my students several years ago that they took a morbid delight in watching a video called "Faces of Death," which shows people's faces as they are dying in various disasters. While my students' voyeurism seemed monstrous to me when I heard about it, I realize now that perhaps they weren't so different from me as I would like to think; maybe that was just their way of trying to come to terms with a basic fact of life that none of us can even begin to understand.

Much of today's articles on health and advertisements for drugs seem designed to convince people that if they will only eat the right foods, get enough exercise, and take the right drugs, they will be able to avoid death altogether. While drug ads picture people enjoying life in the most idyllic environments with soothing music in the background, however, the voice-over is quietly listing the many possible horrendous side-effects of these drugs, often including death. The best way to watch drug ads on TV, I've decided, is with your eyes shut. That way, you can hear what you need to know without being distracted by pretty pictures.

Since death is the end of a life's chronological journey, I have also been preoccupied ever since I can remember with the passage of time. When I was 8 or 9 years old, and people would ask me how old I wanted to be, I would always answer 5 or 6; I had been especially happy during those years and wasn't in any hurry to leave them behind. My obsession with the passage of time has continued to plague me to this very day. I can clearly recall walking down the hall in high school thinking, "I am here today, but soon it will be tomorrow, and today will be gone forever." In my junior year of high school, my speech teacher asked her students to choose a passage to record at the beginning of the semester and re-record at the end to see if we had improved our delivery. More than 50 years later, as I was moving from my home in Oklahoma to an apartment in St. Louis, I found that old vinyl, 45-rpm record wedged down behind a shelf in a piece of furniture that had been traveling around the country with me from one home to another all those years, and I was shocked to hear how vulnerably young I sounded in 1955. But I wasn't surprised to hear the poem I had chosen to read—Edgar Allan Poe's "A Dream Within a Dream?" I found I could easily relate to Poe's imagery of life as a dream, in which the days are like grains of sand, slipping through our fingers despite our best efforts to hold onto them. It was a perfect poem for an adolescent, filled with melodramatic angst. But it expressed my feelings perfectly back then—and still does. Poe, who was a depressive alcoholic drug abuser, died on my birthday (October 7) at the age of 49. I'm not sure what my excuse is for sharing his rather gloomy view of time. Unlike him, I've never tried any illegal drugs—not even pot. I was close to 30 before I had my first taste of alcohol, and I've never been more than slightly tipsy. Perhaps my problem is that I have simply never grown up.

One might think the fact that I have been extraordinarily lucky in not losing any family members or close friends to untimely demise would make an optimist of me. *Au contraire.* It makes me remember a warning my mother used to give to me whenever I did anything to upset her: "Your time's coming!" she would say with unseemly glee. After my children were born, I never dared to sleep soundly, for fear disaster would strike them in the night. Somebody had to be alert. In the early days of my marriage, when Harold was a sportswriter covering games at night and writing them up afterwards, I would fall asleep in the early evening but waken with a start if he hadn't arrived home by 1 a.m.; between then and the time he actually pulled in the driveway, I buried him many times over and had to fight to keep from calling the police to find if there had been any accidents or muggings along his route. In 1968, when he served as press secretary for Paul Simon's successful campaign for lieutenant governor of Illinois, I got attacks of diarrhea every time I took him to the airport, terrified that his plane would crash.

I have never been able to avoid the feeling that my luck can't possibly hold out, so I worry excessively about the safety of my loved ones and the condition of my own (usually excellent) health. If anyone ventures to suggest that worrying doesn't help, I offer as overwhelming evidence to the contrary that I have worried about thousands of things that have never happened, so if I want my luck to continue, I can't afford to stop now.

This obsession with death and the passage of time is perhaps one reason that I have been drawn all my life to old people. During my primary school years, I could often be found in our neighbors' houses, talking to the women while they went about cooking and cleaning. But I had an especially tender feeling for old men, who seemed to me like little boys in old bodies. I was the first grandchild on my mother's side, and very close to my Grandpa Rainbolt. Inexplicably, the same man who had beaten, psychologically abused, and terrified my poor mother when she was growing up took a shine to me immediately, and I to him. A master carpenter and foreman for a construction company, he would come home in the evening and sit in his rocking chair to remove his shoes and socks. If I happened to be there, I would stand behind him and lovingly massage his neck. When he went to the bedroom to prepare for sleep, he often swiped the change off his dresser and handed it to me. He was fascinated by the fact that I, like my father, had been born in Texas, and he called me his "Texas jackrabbit." I loved to whistle, something I had picked up from my mom, and when I did so in his presence, he would say, "Whistlin' girls and crowin' hens always come to some bad ends," but he would say it with a smile—something I doubt that he ever did when my poor mama was growing up. It's a well-known fact that grandparents often mellow, but I think my mother never quite got over how much her dad had changed, and I almost think that the love that flowed between my grandfather and me was a surrogate for the love that neither of them was able to fully express until he was on his deathbed.

I have gradually come to suspect that the fear of death, for me, is really about losing control, a fear that gains in intensity as I grow older and am less and less able to control my own body, let alone the world in which we all struggle to live. I have always been keenly aware of the irony of life—that I can prepare all I want to for disaster, but it's the thing I'm not prepared for that will get me in the end—and that knowledge really ticks me off. The birth of my first child, however, convinced me that I'm not nearly so afraid of death as I am of pain. Not having the advantage of a Lamaze class, an epidural, or an obstetrician trained in natural childbirth, but having read a book called "Childbirth Without Fear," by one Dr. Grantley Dick-Read, I thought I was going to breeze through the birth of my first child with a minimum of pain. Imagine my surprise when I discovered, in the paraphrased words of comedian Bill Cosby, that giving birth is somewhat akin to grabbing your lower lip and pulling it up over your forehead. It wasn't long before I was begging everyone in sight for gas, but the nurses kept putting me off, saying, first, that I couldn't have any until gas the anesthetist came, and then, after he arrived, that I couldn't have any until the doctor got there. When the doctor finally rushed into the delivery room and the nurse put the mask over my face, I took a huge gulp. "Oh! I've taken too much and I'm going to die!" I thought. But the last words I remember going through my head before I blacked out were, "Oh well . . ." So I suspect that fear of pain and resentment over lack of control are two of the major reasons for my obsession with death. The other is just the pure mystery of it all. I like to have answers.

As a result of a lifetime of clean living (if you don't count some risky sexual behavior) and/or good genes, I've made it to my 75th year and appear to have fairly decent prospects of living a good many more—more than I had planned on or saved money for, unfortunately, so that now, while I still worry about dying, I also worry about not dying soon enough. Still, it seems to me that the days have flown by, and I am equally unable to account for how I got to this place in time as I was to imagine my own death when I was a child. While my life has seemed unbearably painful at times (emotionally, at least) and incredibly wonderful at others, it has passed by all too quickly. "Old age is the most unexpected thing that happens to a man," Leo Tolstoi is supposed to have said. Others credit Leon Trotsky with the statement, but whoever said it first, I've no doubt that many an old man has thought it—and many an old woman, too.

The Room

I thought I would never forget anything about that room. As I lay on the bed the night before my 15th birthday, I surveyed it like an archeologist, carefully noting everything: the perfectly smooth white woodwork and the shoulder-high windows that wrapped around the corner, covered by heavy drapes. But now I'm no longer sure about all the details—whether the walls were mint green or beige or the woodwork included fancy scrolled corners or plain miter joints. It was a very long time ago.

I can tell you that the door was opposite the foot of the bed, and I remember watching the doctor's wife coming through it and laying a tray of food on the rolling hospital table that stretched across my bed: a home-made hamburger on Wonder Bread, thick and juicy, but lightly seasoned, along with a glass of milk. "We don't want your stomach to be upset later on," she said.

Her husband had already placed the packing inside me, and she had given me a shot of Vitamin K, "to make sure your blood is clotting properly." There was no phone in the room, and cell phones were still a science fiction fantasy. We had been told that I could not make any calls, and if I wanted to use the toilet, I had to ring a bell for permission. It would be awkward, the doctor's wife explained, if I were to run into another girl in the hall. I had neglected to count the doors on the way in, so I had no idea how many other girls in my predicament might be moving through the house during the next few hours.

He was apparently a real doctor, because I could hear voices of workmen in the basement address him as "doctor," and his wife seemed to be a nurse. The room where he had filled me with the packing and where the procedure would be performed much later that evening was fully equipped with table and stirrups, overhead lights, sink and a gas cone his wife would use to put me under ever so lightly. Through the buzz, I could feel something twisting and turning inside me and hear water running as he washed his hands afterwards.

Now that I know St. Louis better, I think the house was in Clayton or Ladue, since the doctor had picked me up outside the old Clayton Famous-Barr department store, and we didn't drive very far. But I wasn't familiar with St. Louis suburbs back then, being from across the river, in Illinois. I had been instructed to stand alone by the curb and watch for a Cadillac with a monogram on the door. I think the doctor's first name was Morris. His last name started with an "S." I remember what it was, but there are still several people in St. Louis with that name who are prominent donors to cultural institutions, and there's no reason to involve them in my story.

"When did you have your last period?" he asked as we drove away from the department store. When I told him, he slowed down and made a turn, heading back toward the place where he had picked me up. "You're farther along than I thought," he said. "You'll have to spend the night, and it will cost more. Do you think your parents have already left? I'll have to have their OK before I can go ahead with it."

"I don't know. It's just my dad. He said he was going to look around for awhile. Maybe he's still there."

"See if you can find him, and tell him it's going to cost $400 instead of $200, and that you'll have to spend the night. I'll be back out front in 20 minutes."

Dad was in the book department—the first place I headed. Although he appreciated beautiful things, nothing material ever mattered much to him, except books. Often when I saw him tenderly hold an old leather-bound first edition and reverently turn its rag-paper pages, I thought I would be lucky if I ever found anything to love as much as he loved books.

Until a few days before, I had thought I loved Ronnie. Now I wasn't thinking at all, even though I was carrying his baby. On our way to Piggott, Arkansas, in his second-hand Pontiac, Ronnie had given me a wedding ring with a tiny chip diamond in it. We had heard there was no waiting period there, and that girls didn't have to be over 16 to get married without their parents' consent. I was prepared to lie about my age, but when we arrived, we found the rules had changed. There was a waiting period, and blood tests, and you needed a birth certificate. I had no idea where my birth certificate was, and we couldn't afford to stay in a motel three days. Anyway, I knew that within a few hours my parents would have the Highway Patrol after us. So we turned around and drove home through the night, stopping to make love in the car in Olive Branch, Illinois, not speaking about what was awaiting us at home.

That was a week before my night at the doctor's house—a week during which, in mute guilt and shame, I had surrendered my will to my parents. Mom seemed to be running the show, as usual. Dad was a mere shadow in the drama, the pick-up and delivery guy.

"Let me see your breasts," Mom had said, after Ronnie had been banished and I put on my nightgown and crawled into bed. Unlike some of my friends' mothers, Mom never let me see her in her underwear, and she probably hadn't seen my naked body since I had learned to bathe myself, so being commanded to bare my breasts to her only intensified my sense of dreamwalking.

"That's what I was afraid of," she shook her head sadly when she saw my brown, distended nipples. The next day, she drove me to a doctor's office in East St. Louis, where her diagnosis was confirmed.

I refused to wear the white gown when the doctor examined me. If he was going to look at my most private parts, it seemed silly for me to cover up the rest of my body. He didn't argue. A kindly but haggard man with bags under his eyes, hair that fell down over one eye and cigarette smoke clinging to his coat, he told me to put my clothes back on after he finished examining me and called my mother into the room.

"How many times have you had intercourse?" he asked. Mom shook her head sadly when I said I didn't know. He then sent me out of the room to talk to her privately, and a couple of days later I found myself a passenger in another doctor's car, heading toward a strange house in suburban St. Louis. There was an exotic, unfamiliar odor in the car, like I figured Turkish cigarettes might smell if I had ever smelled any.

I'm not sure I had any rational thoughts from the time Ronnie had dropped me off at my house until after everything was over. I must have read a book—I was always reading a book—but I can't remember it. If I missed Ronnie, I don't remember that, either.

It was 1954, and my parents were co-pastors of a tiny Assemblies of God church in East St. Louis, Illinois, a church that didn't believe in sex before marriage or divorce afterwards—and certainly not abortion at any time. Anyway, abortion was still illegal in the United States. If anyone ever found out what Mom and Dad were doing, they would not only lose their church, they would lose their licenses as ministers. And they would probably go to jail. They didn't have to tell me, I just knew.

I don't remember the conversation with Dad in the book department that night. All I know is that I found myself back in the doctor's car, riding along unfamiliar streets. We pulled into an attached garage and entered the house through the kitchen, where the doctor's wife, a friendly, middle-aged woman with black hair, greeted me and led me down a hall to my room. The room in which I lay waiting for the rest of my life to happen.

Take Me to a Place

Oh, take me to a place where love lasts
and friendships never fade,
where loyalty's a given
and mistakes are never made.

Bring back my long-dead parents
and my babies, grown up and gone away,
restore my youthful hopefulness
that all things wonderful would stay.

Grant me a god of eternal love
who can keep us all from inflicting pain,
and give me a new, resilient heart
so that I can love again.

Many Thanks...

Although they have been gone for many years, I must start by thanking my parents, Paul V. Chamless and Mary Ruth Rainbolt Chamless. Both avid readers, they instilled in me not only a lasting set of values but an overwhelming love of books, which led to my desire to be a writer. I thank my little brother, John Chamless, for putting up with his frequently annoying big sister all these years and for the many good conversations we have had about books—especially Russian writers, for which we share a passion. My former husband and the father of my children, Harold Piety, to whom I was married for 20 years and who is still my dear friend, influenced me more profoundly than anyone besides my parents; I still stand in awe of his prodigious knowledge, vocabulary, and mastery of the writer's art. He has generously given me his permission to write anything about our relationship that I feel will help me tell my story. My three brilliant and talented daughters, Tamara R. Piety, Marilyn G. Piety Foley (M.G. Piety), and Julia C. Rieman, who have inherited their father's intellect and skills, have been in my corner every step of the way. They are truly the light of my life.

Without the late Jim Kunde, who gave me my first freelance contract at the Kettering Foundation, and Bob Daley, my first boss at Kettering and still the best boss in the world, my subsequent career as a writer/editor might never have been.

John Hoover, director of the St. Louis Mercantile Library at the University of Missouri-St. Louis, and Dean E. Cody, emeritus associate professor with the Lovejoy Library at Southern Illinois University at Edwardsville, were most gracious in providing documents and information regarding my dad's work at Lovejoy and the collections in his name at both the Mercantile and Lovejoy libraries.

Many, many thanks to Lea Koesterer, my multi-talented and ever-gracious friend and traveling companion, for allowing me to use a photograph of her gorgeous stained glass creation, "Dance of Life," on the cover. I am also blessed to have a very talented young cousin, Lisa Rainbolt Maher, who volunteered to make excellent audio recordings of some of the essays and poems in the book.

My fellow members of the (Un)Stable Writers group in St. Louis—especially Ben Moeller-Gaa, Kristin Sharp, Autumn Rinaldi, Dawn Leslie Lenz, Lisa Ebert, Denise Mussman, and Amy Genova—have given helpful feedback on several parts of the book.

Thanks to all the readers in Stillwater, Oklahoma, who responded positively to my column in the *Stillwater NewsPress*, encouraging me to believe that others might want to read what I write.

And, finally, I thank my dear friends. Trish Macvaugh not only read and critiqued several of the essays; she also took the lovely photo of me and my cat, Daisy. The very talented artist Ron DuBois acted as my unpaid agent by taking it upon himself to send several of my columns to the *Oklahoma Observer* and other publications for reprinting. Sue Cody, Sharon Wright, Fran Sisson and Andrea Jackson have all been kind supporters. And, finally, my dear friend Judith M. Kelly has gone far above and beyond the call of friendship in her support for my writing, reading every word as it came off the computer, goading me to keep writing, and believing in me more, I think, than I believe in myself.

CPSIA information can be obtained at www.ICGtesting.com
Printed in the USA
LVOW08s1056051213

363908LV00002B/179/P